Morning Light

Morning Light

*Wildflowers, Night Skies, and
Other Ordinary Joys of
Oregon Country Life*

Barbara Drake

Oregon State University Press
Corvallis

The paper in this book meets the guidelines for permanence and
durability of the Committee on Production Guidelines for Book
Longevity of the Council on Library Resources and the minimum
requirements of the American National Standard for Permanence of
Paper for Printed Library Materials Z39.48-1984.

Library of Congress Cataloging-in-Publication Data

Drake, Barbara.
Morning light : wildflowers, night skies, and other ordinary joys of
Oregon country life / Barbara Drake.
    pages cm
Summary: "In stories about subjects ranging from training herding dogs, constructing a good well, and neighbors who are careless
in their target shooting, essayist Barbara Drake ruminates on rural
life."—Provided by publisher.
    ISBN 978-0-87071-760-4 (paperback : alkaline paper)
1. Drake, Barbara. 2. Country life—Oregon—Yamhill County.
3. Yamhill County (Or.)—Social life and customs. 4. Yamhill County
(Or.)—Biography. I. Title.
    F882.Y2D73 2014
    979.5'39—dc23
                                        2014030420

Oregon State University Press
121 The Valley Library
Corvallis OR 97331-4501
541-737-3166 • fax 541-737-3170
www.osupress.oregonstate.edu

*To the youngest members of the tribe: Eben, Griffin, Miles,
Delphinium, Mavis, Sadie, Beck, Eliot, Hazel, Logan,
Colin, Stellan, Rowan, Kirun, Rees, Helena, Ian, Stella,
Oliver, Henry Jay, Sienna, Raymond, and Lillian. May your
mornings be bright, your nights full of stars. May the air you
breathe and the water you drink always be sweet and clean.
When it rains let it be a blessing.*

Contents

Preface

I roll over in bed and look at the clock. It's almost 6:30 a.m. As I do every morning, I look east out of the bedroom window to see what kind of day it's going to be. This clear, wintery morning, I see Venus. I know that Saturn is out there but invisible in the morning light. On the other side of the house, Jupiter will have already dropped behind the Coast Range. Only brilliant Venus has the power to shine at this hour.

There is a bed of cottony fog tucked into the neighbors' low-lying cow pasture on the opposite side of the valley. The sun hasn't risen yet, but the sky is turning blood-orange behind the jagged black silhouette of fir trees along the Chehalem ridge. I lie back for a moment, enjoying the prismatic horizon just before sunrise. Orange sky rising to yellow turning to pale green to light blue to darker more violet blue. All in order. It's going to be a good day.

This large, double-paned window with a wide view replaced the small window with the rattling frame that was here when we moved to the farm twenty-six years ago. I remember that first uncomfortable night all too well. It was a hot July, and the open window had no screen. Mosquitoes kept me awake all night. Before dawn I was ready to move back to Portland. I wondered if we had been crazy to buy this wretched house and move to the country where mosquitoes would eat you alive in your own bed.

Now, in the blink of an eye, I am twenty-six years older, and I never want to leave this place.

I pull on my robe and slippers and go out to the kitchen. Guy comes wagging out of the laundry room where we keep his food dish. Maggie appears from the couch in my office. The two border collies and I go out to look around the dark yard—dew on the grass but no frost. The rooster in the dark chicken house hears us and crows dutifully to remind us that he is still in charge. I open the chicken house door, and my feathered dinosaurs race outside. I give them Layena pellets and cracked corn. Besides that, the world is their all-you-can-eat salad bar. Chickens are funny that way. Of course, they eat out of the feed pan, but they are so much more excited if we throw cracked corn, or anything else for that matter, on the ground as a treat. Scratch and peck is a chicken's preferred mode of dining.

Back in the kitchen I put my little Italian espresso pot on the stove and pour milk into a glass measuring cup to heat in the microwave. We are twelve miles from the nearest barista and don't have a fancy espresso machine, but I enjoy my morning latte and use a hand-pumped foamer to give the hot milk that layer of froth that for some inexplicable reason makes a difference. When the coffee is done, I take my caffeinated cup and go to sit with decaf Bill, who is already working the *New York Times* crossword.

Now sunlight pours over the ridge and turns the top oak grove red, while a yellow gloss spills onto the hills and valleys to the south and west. In the distance, the Coast Range is a deep smoky blue. It's a lovely show.

We moved here in 1987. For four years I had been driving two hours a day, to and from our house in Portland to my job at Linfield College in McMinnville. As the kids graduated from high school and college and moved on, we decided it was time to get closer to my job. We loved our Portland house and loved living in the heart of the city, but traffic on my morning commute was getting worse all the time. Some days I felt as if I were a rocket being shot into space or a leaf careening down rapids as I picked up speed, maneuvered on and off freeway ramps, and managed the congested lane changes that would get me to work. Carpooling meant longer days as the carpool members adjusted our times to accommodate everyone's varying schedule. Bill and I decided we would relocate to Yamhill County and move back to Portland when I retired. Now, though I still teach occasional classes, it's been six years since I officially retired, and no one's packing.

Over the years we have been able to check off a long and daunting list of repairs and replacements. The house has been re-roofed, a new foundation added, a new septic system installed, a new well dug, all the windows and several doors have been replaced. Kitchen cabinets have been replaced, gutters replaced, water pipes replaced, new efficient woodstove added, furnace installed to replace the old baseboard heaters... Bill himself has single-handedly ripped out much of the house interior and replaced walls, floors, and ceilings. And then there's the fencing and cross-fencing of pastures, the jobs of installing posts and stringing wires in the vineyard, chopping a winter's worth of firewood each year, looking after livestock, cleaning the barn and chicken house, pruning and general maintenance in the two-acre vineyard, refreshing interior paint from time to time, and putting in and taking care of the vegetable garden. And the day-to-day cooking, cleaning, laundry, trips to town to shop, and general wiping up, all while holding down a teaching job. Beware those of you thinking of moving to the country and rehabbing an old farmhouse. Make sure you know what you're getting into.

Once in a while I wonder whether a day might come when it is all too much. I've noticed that friends around my age or even younger have begun to talk blithely about selling their houses and moving to something smaller and easier to take care of in the city. "Near the kids," they will say. Their kids, like ours, usually live in the city, and this would certainly be the most persuasive reason to move. I would love to live closer to our children and grandchildren, but on the other hand I hope they are glad to have this country place to visit.

My oldest child is forty-nine, a year older than I was when we moved here from Portland. Nowadays, from my perspective as a seventy-four-year old, forty-nine seems like a kid, and time is beginning to feel like a luge race down a very steep chute.

As the years sped by, I fell in love with this roughneck place.

There are many reasons to love country life, among them having dogs. Portland is somewhat a dog city—off-leash parks, a generally sympathetic attitude. But I don't doubt for a moment that life with dogs is better in the country. Border collies Guy and Maggie are our third and fourth farm dogs, respectively. Jack and Mollie, the previous border collies who grew up on this place, lived to be thirteen and sixteen. A friend getting a new dog once said to me, "Do you ever wonder how many more dogs you will have in your life?" I hadn't thought about it that way, but it could be one way to measure your own lifetime. I've had a lot of dogs.

I know city people have dogs galore, but living with dogs seems a better fit with country life. No nearby neighbors to get irritated if they bark. No delicate decisions about which public park or meridian or yard to manage the daily poop-and-scoop ritual. We don't infringe on anyone else's grass. No trips to the dog park for exercise. We have twenty acres. Of course our dogs don't "run free." Only fools move to the country, buy a dog, and let it roam. Our dogs live in the house and come and go with us. If need be, we have a large, fenced backyard, but they rarely need to be penned. Our dogs are never out at night. They only leave the property with us, on our morning walks, or in the car or truck. If we are outside, they sit by the kitchen door waiting for something to happen or walk around with us as we do chores.

And there is the air. Now at the end of fall the rain is back after a long summer drought. The fresh-washed air is like champagne. Even in dry months the air is great. The part of Yamhill County where we live is southwest of Portland, on the other side of a long series of hills. City pollution and seasonal smoke from eastern wildfires move west from time to time, but generally stay on the other side of the Chehalem Mountains. The air is wonderful. Okay, I admit that we sometimes get a scent of the mushroom farm down the road, and when farmers are plowing, planting, or harvesting, dust and pollen and occasionally a whiff of fertilizer taint the air. At such times hay fever sufferers will get watery eyes. We get skunks out this way, too, and their smell can be powerful. But when I talk about air, I am not talking about authentic country smells. I am talking about unpolluted air, the kind that makes it possible for lungworts and other lichens and mosses to drape the trees in the oak woods and beyond with luscious, deep cushions and fronds of green.

Is it silly to say I want to stay in the country because we have lungwort in our woods? Lungwort, or *Lobaria pulmonaria,* is a beautiful macrolichen sensitive to air pollution. It lives on the bark of large, old trees and decaying branches. Lungwort disappears in areas where pollution, habitat loss, and forest practices create an inhospitable environment. It's called lungwort because of its lung-like appearance and also possibly because of its association in folk medicine as having healing properties for asthma. In summer when the air is dry, lungwort turns brown or blackish and shrivels, but when wet weather returns and the falling oak leaves admit light, it opportunistically fills with life, turning bright photosynthesizing-green on the top surface and creamy white on the bottom. That's what it's doing now in November. When the lungwort turns lovely, and seaweed green, I walk the wooded paths and take deep breaths, feeling grateful to live where the air is pure enough for lungwort to thrive.

Another reason for staying here is simply the beauty. On clear days I wake spotlighted in sunshine. Whatever the weather, morning light in the country is infinitely variable, and our broad and distant views allow us to become connoisseurs of light. Depending on atmospheric moisture and air currents, morning clouds can be layered, sparse, voluminous, gray, multi-colored, or absent. We live on a ridge, and no other houses or high buildings block our sky view. We can see thunderheads forming on the other side of the distant Cascades and fog banks lying just across the Coast Range. A blue layer of clouds may appear to be moving south while a peach layer moves north. Even on rainy days, there is apt to be a bright spot behind the clouds that tells us where the sun is as it does its seasonal dance from north to south and back again. On the west side of the house, a rolling landscape filled with tree shapes, farm buildings, misty valleys, and domestic animals shines forth with the detail of an eighteenth-century landscape painting.

Across this temperate landscape, domestic and wild fruit trees blossom in the spring—pink and white wild plums, Italian prunes, a multitude of apples and pears, both planted and wild. Our woods and pastures present a delicate succession of wildflowers and grasses. When the blooming seasons are over, the tangle of dark vegetation and bare trees in the depth of the winter woods reminds me of Arthur Rackham's Victorian fairytale illustrations. The black and white of a rare snow day, fog in distant valleys, tiny iridescent gardens of lime-green moss on aging fence posts—they are all part of the visual feast.

And there is wildlife. Birds. Deer. Occasionally elk. Tiny green tree frogs. The fascinating articulation of praying mantises that are especially abundant in the vineyard. Migrating geese. The wintering-over swans that skimmed low across the driveway one morning. In fall, cedar waxwings come through by the hundreds to strip berries from our wild hawthorns. In winter months, bluebirds arrive to dine on mistletoe berries in the oaks. Today there were a dozen of them swooping between the dark clusters of mistletoe in the oak trees and the birdbath outside our kitchen door. The pileated woodpeckers, often two of them, usually show up spring and fall. Nuthatches peep as they feed upside down on the trunks of the large oaks. Both gray and reddish-brown squirrels whisk away nuts from our walnut trees or scold the dogs from treetops. Horned owls hoot ceremoniously each night before sailing out of the woods to hunt in utter silence.

And then there are the occasions when family and friends visit. Grandchildren run and hide in a maze of paths Bill has mowed in the pasture, or a bonfire above the vineyard makes a warm place to gather on a damp day.

If we moved away from here we would miss all that, as well as generous garden space, fields for livestock, and the quietness of it all. A tiny well-groomed yard or the hired landscape of a condominium could not compensate.

But what if we just can't cope, or can't afford this life? Recently an underground water pipe burst outside the kitchen door. Bill dug a ditch to locate the problem. It needed professional repair, and a plumber told us that an old stretch of pipe connecting newer sections was corroded and falling apart.

Because the water would need to be turned off, we filled buckets for flushing the toilet and filled a pitcher of drinking water. I gathered the laundry and went into McMinnville, where I did the wash at a laundromat and bought eight gallons of bottled drinking water. I went to the gym for my workout and shower. Over the years, we have learned the routine when the water is off for some reason—an electric outage, lines down in a storm, a well or plumbing repair required.

As it turned out, we had to replace not only the broken pipe but a whole line. And the leaking water caused the overworked pump in the well to burn out. Trucks and equipment came in. Pipes were replaced. A new pump went into the well. It was a relief to have the water up and flowing again, but it set us back a chunk of money we hadn't planned on spending. House repairs happen in the city too, but in the country it often feels as if you are more dependent on your own resources.

And surprise! Having lived here for this long, some of the things we did early on now need attention again. The outside cedar shingle siding, put on in 1987, could use a good wash, maybe a stain. The wooden decks we added to the front and side of the house need repainting for the second time. The laundry room needs a new coat of paint. Next spring I'd like to make some improvements to the storage building out back. The soft pine kitchen floor takes a beating from boots, cooking, and dogs' toenails.

The year I was twelve years old I went to five different schools and lived in six different towns. Between 1979 and 1983, when I was trying to make a job move back to Oregon from Michigan, I lived in five different dwellings. I've moved a lot. Here on the farm we recently replaced all our kitchen appliances. Suddenly it strikes me, never before have I lived anywhere long enough for household appliances to wear out. I have never, ever lived anywhere as long as I have lived here.

And yet there are still sometimes those questions: Would it be good for us to move back to the city as we once intended? Live in a neighborhood where we could walk to stores and avoid driving? Should we be closer to doctors and emergency rooms? At seventy-seven, Bill says he's not as strong as he used to be. Sometimes his right knee hurts. He can't kneel on it comfortably. And yet he still chops wood, puts in a garden, tangles with blackberries, keeps the vineyard going, and so far as I can tell he does it all happily. I have arthritis in my thumbs and feet. I can't easily open jar lids anymore. It makes me mad sometimes. If arthritis feels like this at seventy-four, what will it feel like when I'm my mother's age? She's ninety-four and lives on her own, a model of longevity I aspire to. I guess sore thumb joints are not so bad.

I don't feel very old. I write and go to my sociable and support-ive writing groups (two of them). I make good home-cooked food. I can grape and tomato juice at the end of summer. I make jam and chutney. On holidays we often entertain a large crowd of friends and relatives for dinner. Bill and I swim at the college pool in town. On most days we walk the dogs two or three miles, meanwhile admiring the sky, the wildflowers, the birds. There were little gray and yellow finches this morning, lazuli buntings in the summer, a passing small flock of meadowlarks last spring. To see such things you have to be out there, and we are.

I recently heard someone say, everyone wants to live a long time, but no one wants to get old. Newspapers and magazines and tele-vision talk shows are full of advice about how to stay young with exercise, vitamins, weight loss, certain foods or regimens. Maybe one day there will be a pill for old age, but if so the world is going to get awfully crowded. In the meantime, what I want to do is to stay as long as possible in this body, in this lovely, country spot. I can live with the rough edges.

Country life continues to excite and interest me. I love seeing the Ameraucana hens roaming around the yard, and we prize their delicious blue and green eggs. One of the year-old hens decided to hide out and brood in the fall. She hatched a single egg, and we now have a six-week-old chick running with the flock. A feral, marmalade cat with a clipped ear adopted us three years ago. We call him Pinky. Since we quit raising sheep, I miss the roving flock and especially the spring lambs, but who knows, maybe we will go to the auction at the end of winter and buy a few sheep to keep company with Pinknose, our last, old Romney.

The Visitor

I am working the red hand pump over the cistern. Now, in July, water saved from last winter's rain pours into the watering can. Guy, the black and white border collie, snaps and leaps at the gushing water. He thinks it's something he can herd, and flowing water is exciting. When the can is full, I pour it over the red and white geraniums in flowerpots along the porch.

I am happy to have the cistern on our dry hill. Oregon's Yamhill County is suited for oaks and grapes, but it can be difficult to grow softer things with shorter roots. Wells in this area are often chancy and insufficient. On our twenty acres, there are at least four old wells, exhausted and abandoned over the past century. In western Oregon, known for its wet climate and forty-five inches or more of annual rain, it's surprising, but the impermeable character of some soils can make it hard to get a good well. Moreover, most of our rain falls from December to March. To conserve well water in midsummer drought, we use the cistern for small watering chores.

This cistern surprised, puzzled, and even horrified us when we moved here from the city. It was a deep, circular hole in our front yard, about four feet across with no pump or other means of raising the water we saw shining darkly when we looked over the edge. It was covered only by a thin, rotten piece of plywood. We dropped in a weighted line and estimated the cistern to be at least twenty feet deep, probably more. The people we bought the place from had two small children. I wondered what they were thinking. Since the surface of the water was several feet below the top of the concrete lining, there would have been no way for an adult, much less a child, to climb out, if one had fallen in.

We considered filling the hole, but finally decided against it. The cistern must have served a purpose at one time, and so, perhaps, it would again. Bill covered the tank with a heavy wooden platform and drilled a hole, into which he installed a water pipe topped with a red-painted, cast-metal hand pump.

Accumulated rainwater comes off the roof and runs into the cistern via gutters and an underground pipe connected to the house downspouts. Though it sometimes has a stagnant smell, it looks clean and clear and is enjoyed by the small green frogs we often find sitting in the spout of the water can or on the lip of the pump. For years when we had geese, we also used it to fill the plastic goose pond, and in occasional winter power outages, when the electric pump in our main well has shut down, we have carried cistern water inside to flush the toilet. In short, it is a cistern of many uses and never runs dry, though sometimes late in the summer the pump needs to be primed with a bucket of water poured into the top in order to get the suction valve started.

Over the years I often thought how grateful I was for the cistern and wondered who dug it. One summer a visitor to our place brought the answer. I missed him the first year he stopped by, but Bill was home when the white-haired, eighty-two-year-old man came up the driveway and introduced himself as the son of the man who dug the cistern long ago. Our visitor was from Michigan, but he had lived on our place as a child and was making a sentimental journey to Oregon where he had grown up.

The next summer I was home when he came back for another visit, and I was able to ask him about the cistern and other things about the place. He told us his father hand-dug the cistern while his mother stood at the top and pulled up bucket loads of dirt. Even in this land of difficult wells, I could scarcely imagine someone so brave as to dig himself that far down, for water or any other purpose, but I was glad he had, since we had used the cistern many times in small emergencies. Knowing the story behind it made it even more like a gift from the past.

Our visitor lived on the farm for only two years, as a toddler, but when the family moved to Portland, where his father worked, they kept the place until he was in his twenties. The family would come out for weekend picnics, and, to a growing boy, the farm represented a rural paradise. He told us he had never loved any place so much as this one, where the Bohemian farmers, as he called his Czechoslovakian relatives and family friends, spent Sunday afternoons on this hill playing music, socializing, and picnicking.

He returned for short summer visits several times over the next few years, sometimes bringing one of his adult children or a grandchild or two. He wanted them to know the place where he had been a boy. We were always happy to tell him we still loved the place, as he did. And yes, we were still using the old cistern as a back-up water supply.

One summer he brought copies of family pictures taken on the farm as many as eighty years before. There he was, a happy toddler. I studied the photos for familiar images. Though the landscape was more open, the trees smaller, with fewer buildings and fences, I recognized the arrangement of the then-slender young oaks near the house. I saw the ancient pear tree in its youth. I recognized the profile of hills to the east, a profile as familiar as a best friend's. In black and white, on the crest of the hill where our vineyard is now, the Bohemian farmers laughed and played their stringed instruments. The men wore hats, jackets, sturdy pants. The women, their long hair done up under straw hats or pulled back on their necks, wore full-skirted dresses. It looked like such a happy time, no wonder our visitor remembered the place fondly.

For years we exchanged Christmas cards. Last year we didn't hear from him, and he didn't visit this summer. I haven't made inquiries. I like to remember him coming up the driveway, eager to once more share our common love of the land.

We are all just passing through, but I believe there are some places that hold our spirits, like rainwater saved for the hottest days of summer.

The Water Question

❖

About ten years ago, after continuing problems with our old well, Bill and I went to the Yamhill City Council with a request to be allowed to connect to the Lilac Hill Water Association's water line, which ends on the property adjoining ours at the edge of our little oak woods. Lilac Hill, a small cooperative association, buys water from the Yamhill Water District, which serves the town of Yamhill itself. Yamhill takes its water from a dammed-up stream in the Coast Range, and in the past has sold "surplus water" to small water districts that pay to install their own pipes in order to deliver the water to a group of users outside the city limits. Such sub-water districts sometimes have as few as ten households and are typically chary of allowing anyone else to join.

Water is abundant in the winter—above ground at any rate—since we have several rainy months, and last winter broke records for rainfall. But during the summer drought, when months go by without rain, low-flow wells like ours sometimes go dry or deliver only a few gallons a day. Earlier we tried to deal with this by installing a small reservoir and a double-pumping system to fill the reservoir when water wasn't needed. At intervals water in the deep well would be pumped into the reservoir, and from there, when we opened a spigot in the house, pumped into the house system. This would even out the water supply without draining the deep well. It worked for awhile, but this summer our old "main" well has dwindled to a trickle.

After our neighbor formed the Lilac Hill Water Association and got permission to lay pipes and connect several dwellings to the city supply, he called and asked if we would like to join. My heart sank. We had just spent thousands of dollars to make two improvements to the property. One was the reservoir and Coyote pumping system I hoped would solve our water problem and the other was a new foundation for the house. I told him I would like to connect but would have a hard time getting the cash together at the moment. The cost of hooking up to the system, including fees to the city, fees to the water district, and the expense of running the pipe to our property, would also be several thousand dollars. I asked if I could call him back when I got some money together, and he said that would be fine. But before we could do that, the city of Yamhill placed a moratorium on adding any more users to the system. If we still wanted to hook up to the new water district we would have to appeal to the city council for an exception.

At that time, Yamhill had between nine hundred and one thousand inhabitants. Back then it had (and still has) one general store, a post office, a gas station that also sells beverages and a few groceries, a pizza parlor, a Mexican restaurant, a high school (shared with neighboring Carlton), a bank, a grade school, and five churches. Over time, various small businesses have appeared and disappeared in a few other buildings: a notary, a barber, a craft shop, and so on. There's no newspaper, but people generally know what's going on in town, and some news is conveyed by means of a school newsletter.

City limits mean a lot or a little in a rural town like this, depending on circumstances. We live about two miles out of town on a hill and can see the high school and gas station from our driveway. Our post office and zip code are Yamhill. We pay taxes to the school district and our youngest son graduated from Yamhill High School. Our fire department is Yamhill. But because of the way in which water districts are funded and organized, we are outside the Yamhill Water District.

Three different water sub-districts come tantalizingly close to our property. The Cove Orchard Water Association has an easement along the edge of our own land where it runs a water line to the house of an immediate neighbor. The easement was granted before we bought our place. This required installing two miles of pipe between her house and the Cove Orchard water system. At that time, the neighbor told me, she was a single mother with a small child and a bad well. Though it was closed to new applications, Cove Orchard made an exception and let her in. She said she withdrew money from her retirement account and hooked up, paying for all the installation work herself. Thus her water pipe runs all along the south border of our property line, about a thousand feet, but we can't tap into it because Cove Orchard is not adding new water lines and because the existing three-quarters-inch pipe is considered too small for more than one house.

Another sub-water district on Adcock Road is just about a mile from our property across the valley, but that district is also closed to new members. The third option, The Lilac Hill Water Association pipeline, ends at the property that joins the back of ours. So near and yet so far.

The night we and another couple who lived outside the city limits attended the Yamhill City Council meeting with petitions to be allowed to join the Lilac Hill Water Association, another item was on the agenda: to make the "temporary" moratorium against adding any more "outsiders" to the water system "permanent." When someone questioned how "permanent" that was, a council member explained that it was "permanent" until the city council decided by vote that it was no longer "permanent."

Although the council ended up denying our request, we were informed that we could buy seventy-five hundred gallons of water per day from the city, at a cost of thirty-six dollars for each seventy-five hundred gallons, if we could find a way to transport it to our house and store it. We would be allowed to do this because there was "surplus" water in the Yamhill system. In fact, one of the council members explained, all of the water in the subsidiary systems was consider "surplus," unless there should come a time in the future that there was no surplus water, at which time the sub-districts could be cut off.

One of the council members, new to the group, asked the council member to explain the concept of "surplus" water and the mechanism by which this cutting off might be done. The other member faltered and said that there might be litigation, and they didn't want to think about that, but yes, there was a mechanism for cutting off subsidiary water districts should the town itself need all its water.

I meanwhile was trying to imagine how we would get seventy-five hundred gallons of water to our house, and, once we got it there, where we would put it. A very large tank? A really long hose? Perhaps there was a water delivery service such as there is in some of the high desert areas on the east side of the Oregon Cascades.

The discussion was long and painful. The secretary, who had no vote in the matter, sometimes interrupted the discussion with comments about how much the city needed to keep its water. One of the Yamhill City Council members, while moving to deny our request, said with a conciliatory air, "If you were my neighbors, and you needed water, I'd just run a hose from my place to yours." I wanted to tell him, we are your neighbors in the broader sense, so how about it? I continued to wonder about that seventy-five hundred gallons per day. How would it be measured? Did it come from a grotto or sacred cave or from a water vending machine in the city hall? Was it simply drawn from the little garden-hose spigot on the side of the city hall building? Only one member of the board voted to grant us access to the water. The others assumed expressions of helpless regret and avoided our eyes while fiddling with their papers and obviously wishing the process would soon be over.

After the city council turned us down for water, I found myself feeling irritated by the developments I saw on the way into Portland, hundreds of acres of new condominiums and enormous houses built almost overnight on what was once rural land, each with a plush watered lawn and, inside, no doubt, at least three baths, including spa-sized bathing facilities. I have visited Pompeii. These houses reminded me oddly of Pompeii with its ancient ruined bathhouses and open-roofed indoor pools, or impluvia, for catching rainwater. I knew these expanding suburban cities near us were already grappling with water questions. There were proposals to draw water from the Willamette or Tualatin Rivers or to recycle wastewater. Good potable water is not an infinite resource.

Our house was built in 1935, and there was another house that burned before this one was built. The multiple wells on the place told us water had always been a problem here, probably starting about one hundred years ago. We were drawing water from one of the old low-flow wells. The others had been capped or cut off. Maybe it was our turn to sink a new hole in the ground.

One argument Yamhill City Council used to deny our request to join the water system was that the water supply belonged to the city, and those who lived there footed the bill. But there is a substantial fee for the right to connect, and monthly water bills are high. So technically, if we were on their water system, wouldn't we also be paying the bill? Besides, even though we are officially outside the city limits, Yamhill is "our" town. It is our post office, our school, our fire district, our community, our zip code.

The problem reminded me of the Rural Electrification Act of 1935. Before it was passed, rural electrification was considered too expensive and too unnecessary. Imagine if people outside of cities had to provide their own electricity today, one household at a time.

While attending the city council meeting I heard talk of something else going on in Yamhill: development. The planned development would be relatively small, but it would add an estimated thirty-eight houses to the city, a major addition in a town of under a thousand people and one that would require more water use.

Two weeks after we had submitted our petition, there was another city council meeting. This one considered the question of annexing thirteen acres a local landowner wanted to develop into a housing tract. I decided to attend because I wanted to know more

and also was still sore about being turned down for water at the previous council.

There was a larger crowd this time, sixty to seventy people—that's
a lot for Yamhill. The meeting room was overfull, every chair taken,
some people hovering around the door.

Because they expected a long meeting with many speakers, the
council members established a procedure for discussion. Anyone
wishing to speak on the issue had to fill out a form. The reason this
was required, we were told, had to do with the planned order of
presentation. First the petitioner for development and his consultant
would be heard. Then the "pro" speakers supporting the petition
would present their opinions, followed by the "opposed" speakers.
After that, rebuttal from the "pro" side would be heard, and finally
general questions about the whole deal would be taken from what
council members referred to as the "audience." In the word "audience" I heard something of how the event was regarded as a drama,
with the council members and other key figures as actors in that
drama and the rest of us serving as audience to the play that would
soon begin.

After the forms requesting a chance to speak had been collected,
the mayor realized that he had not asked people to mark whether
they were O for "opposed" or P for "pro." There was a murmur
about how to deal with this until someone decided that the mayor
would call out the names on the forms, and the named parties would
reply P or O. As the mayor went down his list, the people calling out
P or O seemed to be voting, though the argument was still to follow.

When the P's and O's were sorted, the proposed developer,
whose land was in question, rose and began to make his case. He
told us his wife's family has been in this area since 1850. His own
family had been here since 1860. Historicity can be a strong argument in the country, at least so far as white settlement goes. The
man said he didn't want to change the character of the town but
would, given the chance, develop his land in a gradual, harmonious
manner that would bring new tax dollars and homes for the youth

of Yamhill, who might otherwise be forced to move away when they became adults. He told us that he had raised cows on his land for a long time, but sometime he might not want to raise cows, and in that event he would appreciate the opportunity to subdivide his cow pasture for the purposes of housing future citizens of Yamhill.

His counselor then rose and described how the developer would thoughtfully and with due consideration for the community take the responsibility for providing the necessary infrastructure for a new subdivision.

Then the P's began. One by one they made their case by saying that the developer was a very nice man. He did seem nice. His present land was originally acquired in a trade and sale when his former land was taken by the city for a new sewer system, including the settling ponds on the south end of town. He thus deserved to be compensated and make money by subdividing his land. They also strongly emphasized that children of the present community, who would one day wish to return to live in Yamhill, might not, in some future time, be able to find housing. They evoked a picture of children turned out at eighteen, having to move twelve miles to McMinnville or Forest Grove. The final argument made by most of the P's was that thirty-eight new houses would provide tax money to enable the district to build a new high school, since the present high school was overcrowded and in poor condition.

Once the P's had their say, it was time to move on to the O's. The first O was a woman, who said that her husband was a developer and that she knew from experience that "gradual" and "development" were not compatible. "No one," she said, "is going to tie money up in roads, sewers, and land, and not try to get a return from the investment as soon as possible." Moreover, she continued, she had recently been involved in a move to a new house in the town. In the course of looking for a larger house, she found that there was no housing shortage in Yamhill. In addition to many available houses there were also a number of vacant lots. A query to the council elicited a response that there were, in fact, thirty-two buildable empty lots in the town. It was interesting to know that people kept track of these things.

A series of O's spoke to the question of livability. I was surprised at the number of people who said they could not bear to see the town change and grow. They spoke of urban sprawl going on all around us. It was true. I agreed with them. But I hadn't expected so many people to see this as a problem. Yamhill was a very small town, and the O's wanted it to stay that way.

I was also surprised at the mixture of voices and accents. There were people speaking with a slight drawl and people with accents that sounded like Vermont, Kansas, Massachusetts, California, and others. Some used colloquial language and others sounded like lawyers or school teachers. Clearly not every family in Yamhill had arrived in 1850.

Suddenly I was startled to hear a speaker referring to me. "How can you consider this annexation when just last council meeting you turned down two people who were begging to be let onto the water district, and you insisted that you were unable to agree to their request because the water hydrants in the city were at an unsafe level of water pressure. Is that true?"

The council members looked at one another.

"Well, is it true? Is it?" the woman demanded.

The whole discussion suddenly veered off on the question of whether there was enough water for fire safety or not. Several other people called for clarification of the question. The public works superintendent was called to answer.

"There's no shortage of water in Yamhill," he asserted in a tone of impatience.

Next the fire chief got up. "We have no shortage of water for the fire hydrants in Yamhill. As long as there is any water in that dam, we have adequate pressure for the fire hydrants. Only once in twenty years has there been too little water for safety. It has not occurred since then. We have plenty of water."

I was fascinated.

Someone else got up to ask if any of the smaller water districts would be cut off if the farmland in question was annexed for additional housing. Contracts with the city stipulated that city supply came first. The lawyer for the city spoke reassuringly. He told the gathering that sub-water districts were common all over the state and that there had never been a situation in the state of Oregon when the water supply to a subsidiary district had been cut off. Yamhill had plenty of water.

The meeting continued. It was at least ninety degrees in the crowded room. The council members decided to submit the question of annexation to the voters and assured those present that there was more than enough water for a new development.

Eventually the request was approved. C'est la vie. As for us, we would have to figure things out on our own.

The Dowsers

❖

I was still mulling over that Yamhill City Council meeting—it's frustrating not to get what you want and need—but I pushed the problem to the back of my mind and went with Bill to a party in the nearby Red Hills.

The party was at the home of a couple just getting into the wine business. They lived at the end of an unpaved and bumpy road, which winds up above the Chehalem Valley and provides a view of hills beyond hills, mountains beyond mountains, a rich layering of greens, purples, blues, and gold, romantic and idyllic as art in a dentist's office. But here it was real.

The Red Hills is a local viticulture area named for the red-tinted Jory soil. Jory underlies old forestland that at some time in the past was cleared of native fir and oaks in order to grow crops such as hazelnuts, grain, and Christmas trees. The forests of the past had laid down a thick, organic layer of soil referred to confusingly as silty clay loam. The term silty clay loam also applies to the Hazelaire and Willakenzie soils on our own place, though it all seems like clay when I'm trying to put in a garden or bury a chicken that has gone on to her reward. But silty clay loam is a highly variable soil designation that refers to a mix of these materials in various percentages. Our silty clay loam is not red, though it is also good for wine grapes. In many places around the county, where the land slopes toward sunlight, Jory soil is now being planted with wine grapes. Our hosts were planning for a winery in the future. For now they had twenty-four acres in vinifera grapes, which they sold to other local wineries.

The rustic, locavore picnic featured beef heart shish-kabobs and pit-barbecued goat. Everyone brought "a dish to pass," and the table soon filled up with cole slaw, potato salad, scalloped potatoes, and rice and pasta dishes. An array of desserts included my blackberry pudding and someone else's pecan pie. Someone had brought a bushel basket full of cantaloupes from their garden, the most fragrant and delicious cantaloupes I had ever tasted. And of course there were local pinot noir and chardonnay wines.

Coincident with our own water concerns, the next week our hosts were digging a new well. They were nervous. Their present water supply was two gallons per minute. It worried them that the well digger had asked them to pick the site. "It's up to you to tell me where to dig it," he told them. He was the expert, but wells are tricky, their outcomes uncertain, and in the end the owner of the property must take responsibility for choosing the spot to drill. Water, at least in our neighborhood, doesn't just lie beneath the earth's surface in an evenly distributed reservoir. Its presence depends on the hidden, prehistoric landscape below: volcanic, sedimentary, or ancient ocean beds. Even a few yards one way or the other can mean success or failure.

Wells seemed to be on everyone's mind. We were sampling someone's homemade mozzarella and spreading pita bread with garlicky humus when I started listening to yet more people talk about having a new well dug. The one they had smelled and tasted bad and had low output. They were also starting a vineyard and would like more water to help get the vines started. To choose the well site they had appealed to a neighbor, who also happened to be a dowser. He offered to find a spot for them when they were ready.

Dowsing, also called divining or well-witching, is an ancient tradition, considered magic by some, science by some, and sheer idiocy or fraud by others. Of course, digging into the earth and coming up with water can seem magical where water supplies are erratic, even in an area like ours which is famous for long rainy seasons.

We exchanged phone numbers with these people. We might need a dowser, too.

A week after the picnic, while we were still dithering about whether to try for a new well and where to put it, a dowser traveling through from Iowa called us. He said he was in our neighborhood and had heard we might need his services. Earlier, we had been talking with John, a well driller in our area, and he brought up the subject of dowsing. John had recently met a father-and-son team of dowsers visiting the area. We asked him to have them call us, and now here they were on the phone. The dowser told us the deal: they wouldn't charge anything unless we got at least five gallons a minute. Then the fee was $650.

Bill was convinced we ought to try it. I was surprised, because Bill is a born skeptic on the Scandinavian side, while I am of the Celtic persuasion and would like to believe in magic, or at least a correspondence between natural forces, like ESP and that water flows downhill.

I had known one dowser. When I was growing up in Coos Bay on the southern Oregon coast, there was a neighborhood dowser, a tall, gaunt fellow who walked around wearing a long black coat and carrying a lumpy, heavy-looking backpack. No one questioned who or what he was. He was simply the dowser, or well witch. The dowser lived somewhere out near Empire, which was at least six miles from downtown Coos Bay, and he didn't have a car. He lived in a hand-built house my sister remembers as being made mostly of tree bark, a sort of South Coast Tom Bombadil. You could tell just by looking at his dusty trousers and worn coat that he wasn't getting rich in the trade, but his humble appearance tended to impart credibility. Dowsing was his calling, whether it was profitable or not, and as he walked down the road with that pack on his back he had the air of one who had miles to go before he sleeps.

I had tried dowsing with a Y-shaped tree branch and with bent wire hangers, two versions of dowsing tools. Some South Coast neighbors showed me how to use both. I swear I felt a definite pull. The Y-shaped, fresh cutting from a willow or alder seemed to spin in my hands as the handle of the stick bent downward. Or the wires swung and crossed no matter how hard I tried to keep them immobile. The movement might have been unconscious, or sweat on my palms, but it felt as though some other power were working through my hands.

The trouble was, I'd never had the chance to dig a well where I felt the pull; I had never had a way to confirm my instincts or the response itself. Now, as I looked out over our water-scarce acreage and tried to intuit a likely spot for a new well, witching seemed as likely as anything. We engaged the father-and-son dowsers from Iowa and looked forward to their arrival.

Lanny, a young man in his thirties or early forties, was accompanied by his father, an elderly man wearing a large canvas hat to shield him from the intense summer heat. Lanny's father was small-boned with a weathered, Irish-looking face and reddish tinged eyebrows, though his last name did not sound Irish. The father wore a colorful shirt, and his pants were cinched in with a broad belt on his small waist. Oddly, he apologized for the hat and said something to the effect of, "I don't look so good in this hat." When I said he looked fine, he looked me in the eye and asked, "Do you really think so?" With that dainty waist and pretty shirt he was perhaps a bit of a dandy.

Theirs was no simple stick-and-coat-hanger operation. Lanny explained that he would locate the best place to drill by using a magnometer, which marked out magnetic fields created by iron filings flowing in water over a long period time. His family had been in the actual drilling business in Iowa for many years. In college he became a geologist, but he said his dowsing system—using the magnometer and a computer program to show the magnetic patterns in the earth—was something he devised himself.

They drove their car through the pasture gate and parked in the shade of a small oak grove. As it turned out, the first step in the business had nothing to do with magnometers or computers. Tradition prevailed as the father started wandering around the farm with a piece of bent wire in his hands. He walked quickly up and down various slopes, zigzagging here and there.

Lanny, meanwhile, went to work assembling the magnometer, a gadget he wore on a harness over his shoulders. It had a metal pole extending up and out behind him, and a microphone-shaped device on the end. He began to walk where his father indicated. After they had done this for a while, they fetched rolls of string and orange flags from the car trunk and marked out an area about one hundred meters square on the west side of the place. Then, with some general idea of where they felt the magnetic response, Lanny began to walk back and forth across the field while entering numbers into an electronic-looking box suspended across his chest.

I wondered if we were being gullible, but like the Coos Bay well witch, Lanny and his father didn't really seem to have much to gain from traveling all this way and taking the time to do this. Lanny was clearly fascinated by the possibility of working out a good scientific system for finding water. His father, too, seemed committed to it. And I liked them. They were good people.

In case they'd overlooked something, I offered to show the father around the east side of the place. All the old wells on our property were either on the central ridge or the ten acres on the west side of the farm. I wondered, why not on the east ten acres? I also wondered if Lanny and his father were favoring the open field on the west side just because it was easier to get to. The eastern half of our farm is heavily planted with the vineyard, and covered with wild fruit trees and an oak forest. There is no current road access. But the old man obligingly took his dowsing wand and followed me down through the vineyard and into the wild apple grove. He said he didn't pick up any strong vibes in that area and didn't feel that there was much there. Previously he had walked around our two old, insufficient wells and said that he didn't feel much of anything there either, but he really thought there was something out in the front sheep pasture. His conviction was impressive.

As we walked along, he sampled some wild apples. He told me he liked these "real" apples better than the store-bought apples, which didn't have any taste. He also tried some of the small, yellow-and-red wild plums. He liked those, too, but he especially liked the dark blue Italian plums above the vineyard that were deliciously ripe right then. I got a sack from the house and picked a bag for him.

Then I asked what he felt in the dowsing rod, and he offered to show me.

His device was simply a piece of clothes hanger wire twisted in the middle into a small loop and then bent so that the two arms made a forty-five degree angle. He held the ends of the wire between thumbs and forefingers with the loop turned upward. As he walked over a strong spot, he felt the corner or loop of the wire pull toward him. We went out in the field, where Lanny was still marching back and forth punching his numbers into the machine. "You've got to hold my hand to feel it," said the elder dowser. I held his left hand with my right hand, while he held one end of the dowsing rod in his right, and I held the other in my left. Hand in hand, as if in pastoral bliss, we wandered slowly down the field. I did feel something as we got near an area that he said was strong for water. The tip of the rod turned back toward us. He offered to let me try it by myself, but even though I had felt the pull of dowsing before, this time, when I was not holding his hand, I didn't get any response. "Not everybody can do it," said the old man. I felt a little dejected.

All afternoon in the hot sun, Lanny worked at mapping out magnetic fields. Several times he started over, saying that there was something near the fence that disrupted his calculations. He wondered if there was something buried there or what. So far as we knew, there wasn't, though our neighbor's water line, attached to the Cove Orchard Water Association, passes beneath the land on the outside of our fence. And, of course, there was that mysterious large cable recently buried deep along the other side of our obscure gravel road. As near as I could figure, its purpose was to rapidly send stock market information across the Pacific ocean between Japan and Wall Street. There were also electric and phone lines overhead. Though outside any water district, we were amazingly surrounded by other people's gear for moving water, electricity, and information.

Lanny said the disturbance he felt couldn't be any of those things. They were not close enough. By the end of the afternoon he had given up. He said he'd have to redo his survey and would start again the next day. So far the two men had spent at least five hours with no guarantee of reward.

The next morning they arrived and redrew the quadrant, setting it away from the fence some but still arranging it so as to include the area they were most interested in. After several hours of walking around on an even hotter day, Lanny had his figures. They pounded a metal T-post into the spot where they thought we should dig and tied a red flag on it. Then Lanny came in the house, leaving his father to put away the equipment, while he explained what he'd found and showed us some contours on the screen of his laptop computer. The area he had picked out was near what he called a diamond, a dark area where several possible watercourses converged.

We talked some about wells he'd dowsed. There was a hundred-gallon-a-minute well, he told us, in the schoolyard of a small town notorious for its lack of water about ten miles from our home. He also told us about a well on a mountain outside Carlton that was still in the process of being drilled. They had fourteen gallons a minute so far, and they were going deeper because they were still in a shale formation, a good sign. We talked some more about wells and water. He said he couldn't promise our new well wouldn't be salty—there were old ocean beds deep below the ground—but he really thought there was a good supply of some kind of water where they'd marked it.

It was nerve-wracking to think of putting money into a hole in the ground that might not amount to anything. Once we'd picked a spot, the well driller would charge us about $4,000 to drill and case a two-hundred-foot well. If it came up dry we would "only" pay half the price. Not much consolation. After the drilling costs there would be the expense of laying new pipe and an electric wire to the pump. A reservoir and a system to regulate flow into a storage tank would add at least another $4,000. It could all easily come to between $12,000 and $20,000. I wasn't worried about the dowser's fee. If we really did come up with a five-plus gallons per minute well, the $650 would be a small sum in the total cost.

Since we hadn't been able to connect with any existing system, we needed to commit to drilling this well and paying for it, and in the meantime we needed to get on somebody's schedule. This was the driest time of the year when wells commonly failed, and also the time of year when trucks and equipment could get out to sites without getting stuck in the mud. Everybody was extra busy. It was hard to get a driller to return your call.

The next morning I was surprised to see Lanny and his father drive back up the driveway. "What's up?" I asked.

"Oh, he just wanted to check something else," said Lanny, nodding his head at his father, who had taken off with his dowsing rod and gone back down in the field. No hand-holding, plum-browsing nonsense today, this was serious. The day was even hotter than the previous two. Lanny meandered around while his father apparently refined his observations. They also had Lanny's brother with them this time. He walked down the field carrying a wire rod.

"Are you a dowser too?" I asked him. He looked embarrassed.

"No, I can't make it work," he admitted. "I'm just fooling around here."

I went to the house to get my camera and then went out to take their picture, something I'd wanted to do the day before but had forgotten. When I asked the old man if I might take his picture, he said, again, that he didn't think he looked so good in the hat, but I told him he looked fine. He had on an especially nice shirt with dark blue flowers that looked custom made. The man definitely cared about appearance. He let me take his picture as he wandered up and down the hill. Then I took a picture of Lanny and his dad both together. It was getting so hot, I went back in the house to read and get out of the sun.

After a while the three of them piled back in the car and drove off. They hadn't moved any of their flags and poles. Apparently everything checked out. Now it was up to us to get the well driller on the job. Oh, boy.

The Well

We called John, who told us that he was booked about four weeks out, but he was scheduled to drill a well near us tomorrow and maybe he'd stop by to check out the site we'd settled on. He added that the people he was supposed to drill for needed to put in a gravel road first, and they might not be finished. If he couldn't get in there yet, he would set up at our place instead.

I was antsy about this. Stories about iffy wells were rife in this area. Some people near Gaston got nothing but salt water and had to put in an expensive reverse osmosis or desalinating system to make the water drinkable. Other people near Cove Orchard got only a gallon and a half per minute but were putting in a reservoir anyway because they had no alternative. Then there were the people who got eighty gallons a minute in a place famous for dry wells, and the guy down the road who had four wells drilled in a row, at one hundred yard intervals, and got one dry, one salty, one muddy, and one good one.

As I drove to and from work the next day, I listened to the state news on the radio, and it seemed to be all about water. Wilsonville, a booming suburb of Portland that was once just a sleepy ferry town, wanted to vote on taking drinking water from the Willamette River. Tigard, a large suburb nearby, had decided not to go for the river water for now. At this time of year and at this point in the century, it seemed nobody had enough water. At the Yamhill City Council, meeting someone had claimed that the average household needed about one thousand gallons of water per day. That sounded like a lot to me. I'd heard figures more like 75 to 150 gallons a day per person, but of course it depended on how many times you flushed the toilet, how much your livestock was drinking, how often you washed your car, whether you were irrigating a kitchen garden or field crops, whether you had a hot tub or a pool, or whether you left the water running when you brushed your teeth.

I thought about the various old decommissioned wells on our place. People needing water had been living here for almost a hundred years. We planned on staying.

On my way home from work the following day, I was startled and excited to see that when I turned off the highway onto Russell Creek Road there were three trucks loaded with well-drilling apparatus: a big rig with the drilling equipment, a smaller one with various kinds of tools and pipe, and a flatbed with sacks of the expanding material used to seal a well around the casing.

I followed them slowly, peering through the dust that the huge trucks kicked up on our dry gravel road. It had been another really hot day, in the nineties, and I was sweating as I turned the corner, hoping that they were going to our house. Sure enough, with some difficulty they made the tight turn and pulled over on the right side of the driveway where it ran through the walnut grove. I went past them on down the drive and parked. Bill walked up and told me that the other customers hadn't finished their road, so the drillers were going to do our job first. They would park here tonight and be back the next morning to start work.

The drillers arrived around 8:00 a.m. and started setting up the rig. I wanted to hang around and see how it was done and wished I didn't have to go to work, but wells aren't free so off I went.

During my lunch break I called home, but the line was busy. I tried again. It rang, but Bill didn't answer. So I talked to the answering machine and asked whether they were getting anywhere. Then I went to teach my afternoon class. After weeks of hot weather, it was clouding over, and while I was teaching I looked up and saw a sprinkling of rain in the air that surprised me. Maybe nature was sending a favorable omen. After class, I went back to my office and found an e-mail from Bill. It said there was just a dribble of water at 140 feet, and the drillers were going deeper. I finished a few things in my office and decided to leave an hour early. I was dreading a dry well and calculated just how much it was going to cost and whether there was any way we could cut our losses, such as having John try another spot while they were still on the place.

I felt anxious as I drove into our driveway. There was a damp smell in the air, either from the light rain an hour ago, or from the drilling process, but the ground looked totally dry. Bill was out in the field with the drillers.

"They're at 240 feet," he said, "and they're getting five gallons a minute."

I let out my breath. It was not a lot, but at least it wasn't a dry hole. I thought gratefully of the dowsers. Five gallons a minute would be enough for us if we put in a two-thousand-gallon reservoir and two pumps, one in the ground and one in the reservoir, to even out the use.

In the field there was a slew of wet, gray muck, clay and shale drillings from the hole. The drillers were running a bailer test. John wanted to stop at 240 feet. They had come through a series of fractures that pushed up the water production, but now they seemed to be drilling into a different layer. John was afraid if they went any deeper they'd push through into something else, possibly salt and old seabed. I remembered that Lanny had suggested we drill 300 feet, but his father said 240.

The bailer test, which confirms the flow, involved pumping water out of the hole and measuring how long it took to fill a five-gallon bucket. The drillers did this for an hour because the flow usually falls off after the first pumping of the "charge." John told me that it actually started at about six gallons a minute and now was down to about four and a half and steady. "One minute and six seconds to fill the bucket," he said.

I wanted to taste the water, so John filled a large plastic cup from the well head. Since it had just been drilled, there was gray silt in it, but it wasn't bad. I swallowed. It tasted good, very neutral. No salt. No sulfur taste. It didn't seem as cold as I'd have expected but that was probably because of the air being forced down the shaft to drive the water to the surface.

It was tempting to think of going farther and farther down, just to see what one would find, but I didn't want to lose the okay well that we'd apparently got. So I agreed with John and Bill that we should stop at 240 feet. It was a relief to have water there.

Later that night, after we came home from the Native Plant Society meeting, Bill said he was feeling a little let down that the well didn't have more water. He had been hoping for an impressive success due to the intuition or skill of the dowsers. But even they couldn't put more water where it wasn't.

The whole drilling process fascinated me. What if you could just drill and drill and drill, and see what happened, never mind the cost or consequences, until something at some great depth stopped you and that was it. I was looking forward to talking to my geologist brother about it. I could understand his lifelong fascination with geology and his work on developing oil wells. We were thinking in hundreds of feet. He was used to thinking in thousands of feet. Despite our knowledge of geology, hydrology, soil layers, and so on, the deep earth was a mystery. Often my brother prospected an oil well, and it paid off. But sometimes, even when the research looked good, the results weren't enough to bother with. I wondered what was the depth of his deepest well. Two hundred and forty feet wasn't very deep, geologically speaking. Maybe we should have gone for three hundred. Bill and I both wondered about that extra sixty feet. I was tempted but inclined to let the driller's opinion stand.

And now we had a new well. A lovely thought that had not yet quite sunk in. A new well. The recorded, official flow figure for the records was four and a half gallons per minute. Two hundred and seventy gallons an hour. Six thousand four hundred and eighty gallons in twenty-four hours. It sounded like a lot of water to me, especially since we'd become accustomed to showers running out halfway through and the faucets dribbling when we had a house full of visitors.

Now we had to hire someone to hook up the well with a submersible pump, lay an electrical line and pipes to the water line, install a pressure tank and a pumping system to run the water off and on into a reservoir when we were not using it, and dig the reservoir itself to store water. I wondered how big the reservoir should be, how big it could be. Our other reservoir, a heavy plastic tank we had attached to the old well, was supposed to hold fifteen hundred gallons, but someone made a mistake and brought a smaller tank than we'd ordered. After it was installed, we realized that the company had charged us for a fifteen-hundred-gallon tank and put in a thousand-gallon tank. Yet it was such a relief to have water again that we told them to forget it. We'd deal with the smaller tank if they refunded the difference, which they did. But later, when we looked at the way they'd set up the flow valve, we realized that we didn't even have a thousand gallons of water in storage—more like seven hundred—and the plastic sides of the tank began to slump inward after a few years.

Now it was possible to get a cement tank with a plastic lining. We would choose that, though it would be more expensive than the heavy plastic. Also, I wanted to make sure it had a neck so that we could check it without digging out the tank. The opening on the other small tank had been buried in the ground. Whenever it needed to be checked, or the pump needed work, it had to be uncovered with a shovel. Eventually we added an extension, a cylinder glued into the opening of the main tank, which protruded above the ground, but I was never happy with the way the lid was so low. There was a chance of groundwater seeping into the tank if the seal leaked in a heavy rain. I wanted to make sure that this tank wouldn't have those problems.

When I was driving home from work the day the well drillers were on our property and wondering if they would hit water,

I began thinking of my Catholic girlhood. Who was the saint of water? Who might one pray to that the well would turn out okay? I couldn't think of anyone but Saint Christopher, bearer of the Christ child across water, but I also knew that Christopher had been demoted to apocryphal. Still, throughout my childhood I had worn his medal around my neck, so I sent a small prayer to Saint Christopher that water might be brought to us. Then I thought of my maternal Irish grandmother with her pantheon of saints arranged on the living room mantle. It struck me. Saint Jude. He was her favorite saint, the saint of impossible causes. "Okay," I thought. "Saint Jude, help us out here, in memory of my good grandmother."

As I was thinking of saints, I also remembered our travels in Ireland and the various holy wells, where water ran from rocks and pilgrims placed votive candles to flicker in the grottoes and at the blessed source. No wonder they named them holy wells. Surely water is a blessing.

It was on this train of thought that I rounded the corner. "Okay, Saint Jude," I said. "Here we go." And I drove up the driveway, worrying about the earlier message that there was only a dribble at 140 feet, and I parked, and I walked down the field, and Bill came up and said, "It's good and still pumping."

Although getting a productive well was a happy outcome, it wasn't the end of this particular water story. Because the official record for the well was four and a half gallons per minute, Lanny and his father refused to take their $650 finder's fee. We had a little debate about it. I said I wanted to pay them anyway, but they insisted this would take the credibility from their offer. "I'll just take some more of those plums as a payment," said the old man, and he did, collecting them in a brown paper sack I took out of our bag drawer.

Digging the well was just the beginning. We still had to get water from a hole in the ground to our house's plumbing system. That meant hiring someone else to put in the pipes, electricity, pumps, and tank that would supply the house, a big job. The total cost of our water project was around $15,000. No doubt it would be more today.

This was still not the end of the story, and perhaps it never ends. After a few months the water developed a slight taste of something like salt. It wasn't too bad. Bill said he couldn't taste it, but I did. Whatever the odd mineral, the water worked for baths, showers, and laundry. There was no problem making soapsuds, no apparent residue, but the taste was definitely off. On account of this I bought bottled drinking water, and we used water from the old, slow well and the cistern for watering plants and the vegetable garden.

Eventually we installed a reverse osmosis system complete with one drinking water faucet to provide filtered drinking water inside the house. The system cost about $500, rarely needs new filters, and provides about eight gallons of purified drinking water a day.

Someone hearing about this relatively simple solution mentioned to me that it should be easy, then, for people around the world to make potable water from salt water. Unfortunately, it's not. There are always tradeoffs. Reverse osmosis's drawback is that for each purified gallon gained, water is lost in the filtering process. As nearly as I can tell, our system requires around three gallons of water to make one gallon of drinking water. Some reverse osmosis systems throw away even more. At our small scale, a few gallons flushed away may seem insignificant, but imagine desalinating sea water for a large city like Los Angeles or New York or even a small town like Yamhill. I have no idea how that would actually work, but salt or other minerals and contaminants taken out of water to make it potable have to go somewhere else. Where would that somewhere else be? Nothing really goes away. It is all a sort of puzzle, like the continuing problem of where human societies put their garbage and sewage. Municipal water systems, depending on the quality of their water source, use up all sorts of resources in the process of providing water to cities, but seldom do customers realize how complicated it is to provide the treated water that pours so readily from their faucets or how fortunate they are when the water source is clean and economical.

For now, we seem to have solved our water supply problems, but I can never get too smug about it. Nor can I see a picture of a farmer anywhere in the world staring at his drying crops, or one of disaster victims standing in line with buckets to beg a little drinking water, without feeling that we are all potentially in that dry place, whether due to overpopulation, climate change, pollution, or political boundaries drawing lines between "your water" and "my water." My parents lived through the dust bowl years in Kansas, and it profoundly affected their lives. More than one western rancher has been shot over water rights. More than one child has died due to unclean water. The water we drink from our well has never seemed more precious to me.

Living With Oak Trees

❖

I first read T. S. Eliot's long poem, "The Waste Land," as an English major at the University of Oregon. It was an eye opener for a girl from edge-of-the-continent Coos Bay. To better understand the poem and its allusions to pre-Christian mythology, we read bits of Sir James George Frazer's *The Golden Bough.* Frazer was a Glasgow-born, nineteenth-century anthropologist who wrote about early religion, including prehistoric Celtic practices of making human sacrifice to oak trees. It was all morbidly fascinating, and for a while we creative writing students saw regeneration myths everywhere we looked. Years later, I had reason to remember those mythologies when I learned that big oak trees can be dangerous as well as beautiful.

On our farm we have two separate oak groves consisting of small- and moderate-sized trees and a scattering of larger, more solitary trees, including a few near the house.

One dark Christmas night our home was full of visiting relatives. It had been raining for days, maybe weeks. There are many kinds of Oregon rain: clattering, warm rain that comes in big loose drops; showering rain like glittering vertical threads stitching sky and earth together; freezing rain that coats the world with shimmering ice and sends tree limbs and electric wires crashing to the ground; and the kind of intermittent, barely falling, misty rain my mother always called "spitting." The rain on this Christmas night was a true Oregon deluge, the kind that blows endlessly sideways from the southwest and turns winter mud to jelly, then soup. When such rain saturates the ground there are mudslides on Coast Range roads, and houses slide down sodden banks. Then the earth cannot absorb another single drop, and rainwater pools in broad shining puddles on the surface of lawns and driveways, fields and country roads.

In spite of the torrential rain it was comfortable in our house. There was a cheery fire in the wood stove. We had colored lights and warmth, good food, and the pleasure of gathered family. Late in the evening, many family members who lived nearby had gone home, but there were a dozen who came from out of town and had chosen to spend the night in beds, on couches, or in sleeping bags on the living room floor.

I was suddenly awakened at about 6 a.m. the next morning by dishes rattling on the shelves. The whole house was shaking, and for a few seconds I thought it was an earthquake like the big "Spring Break Quake" we felt on the morning of March 25, 1993. Suddenly there was the explosive, booming sound of something enormous and heavy hitting the ground, as if a passenger jet had fallen into our yard. In seconds, everyone was out of bed. We ran to the front windows and looked outside. There we saw the three fallen trunks of our largest oak, splayed in three different directions, each lying on top of a flattened car. It was a stunning sight, and for a moment we simply stared. In the pre-dawn darkness it felt unreal to see the massive, old tree lying across the destroyed vehicles, its jagged branches filling the yard. We knew it was a big tree, but until it came down we never could have imagined it would cover so much ground. My Taurus station wagon, my daughter's new Ford Ranger pickup, and my stepdaughter's little silver Honda had all been flattened.

The words went across my brain like news headlines on a reader board or the belt of the Brave Little Tailor in the old fairytale: Three cars at one blow! My God, what if someone had been out there when the tree fell!

That day workmen came and went, sawing the fallen trunks into slabs, pulling the heavy wood off cars, repairing the electric line that had gone down with the tree. There was a parade of insurance adjustors, car rental servicemen, and tow trucks. It would be weeks before the yard was cleared, but a few days later, after the largest debris was gone, I called an arborist and had the other trees near the house trimmed and checked for decay and balance.

Since then, I've never felt quite the same about our splendid oaks, especially those that are over one hundred or two hundred years old, massive and long limbed. I thought of those ancient Celtic sacrifice rituals. We had been unbelievably lucky that no one was out in the driveway at the time.

And yet the oaks had wonderful associations too. I remembered my son and daughter-in-law at their wedding almost twenty years ago as they took their vows below the long, graceful limb of one of the old trees in the upper grove. Its limb was decked in flowers and ribbons; the crowd of guests sat on folding chairs beneath other branches. I thought of the shade and beauty of the fallen tree. It had been a magnet for birds, especially the tiny brown creepers and the upside-down-walking nuthatches. One winter we found the delicate hanging pouch of an oriole's nest on a low branch. Squirrels loved that tree.

When the three trunks had been sliced into rounds, I tried to count the rings, but they were so tight and close together I kept losing count somewhere around 160. It was older than that. I wondered if those three trunks were part of one tree or if three trees had grown simultaneously from three different acorns. They seemed joined at the base, but perhaps they had fused over the years.

Sometime later I read Aldo Leopold's essay "Good Oak" in his book *A Sand County Almanac*. He wrote about an oak that had died on his property: "The stump, which I measured upon felling the tree, has a diameter of 30 inches. It shows 80 growth rings, hence the seedling from which it originated must have laid its first ring of wood in 1865, at the end of the Civil War."

Leopold described his tree as a black oak. The ones on our place are Oregon white oak, or Quercus garryana. After reading Leopold's passage, I took a measuring tape out to our largest remaining oak tree, which resided on the hill above our barn, spreading its gigantic limbs. I laid the sixty-inch tape around the trunk of the oak at ground level. It was not long enough. I moved it, and then moved it once more, till I had returned to the starting place. At ground level, where the tree stretched its gnarled roots, the oak's circumference was around 180 inches. At about the level of my chest, where the trunk tapered to its upright form, the tree was a pinch over thirteen feet in circumference. I estimated its diameter to be approximately 50 inches. If this was comparable to Leopold's oak, our tree—so old, could it properly be called "ours?" —was as old as Oregon, which achieved statehood in 1859. Oregon's historic Champoeg State Park, where we often walk, is full of young and old oak trees, some of which must have sprouted about the same time as our old oak.

Leopold described the death of his tree by lightning. He left it standing to season for a year before he cut it down and began to saw it up for wood. As the saw cut into the wood, he imagined the history each ring represented: the time when his family "learned to love and cherish this farm;" the time of the previous owner, a bootlegger, who exploited the land and left it depleted; and all the earlier events through which the old tree had lived. He named events such as the planting of smelt in the Great Lakes in 1909 and the extinction of the passenger pigeon in 1899. He mentioned drought, fire, economic boom and bust, logging, the introduction of non-native grasses in 1879, the introduction of factory-made barbed wire in 1874, and the 1860s, "when thousands died to settle the question" of secession.

Then Leopold cut it up for firewood.

Our car-smashing oak went the same way; oak makes great firewood. Later on, a few years after the ruin of our driveway oak, one of the big oaks above the barn died. It didn't fall; it just didn't leaf out one spring. The oak stood in a thriving grove, and there was no clear reason why it died. Perhaps the cause was root rot, which is exacerbated especially by years of heavy rain and where there is poor drainage. Roots of oaks need to dry out in the summer months to keep them healthy. Root rot is also present in areas that are watered during the dry months, such as the college campus where I taught for many years. Linfield College, a small, private, liberal-arts college, used a spreading Oregon white oak as its symbol on stationery and other materials. Over the twenty-four years that I worked there, each winter at least one or two of the old oaks in the grove fronting the highway would suddenly fall. I had even seen one fall as I was looking at it from my office window. Though these trees looked fine, their roots had grown too weak to hold the aged trees upright when the ground was sodden. One reason was that the area beneath the trees had been tended as a lush green lawn, creating an image people loved for the way it conveyed a sense of tradition, privilege, and beauty. But the summer watering was actually cultivating fungus that weakened the trees' foundation roots. When the college realized what this was doing to the trees, the gardeners started a new regimen of letting the ground dry in late summer to kill or subdue the fungus. Some passersby who saw the sere and flattened late summer grass beneath the trees called the school to complain about the unsightly lack of watering, only to be told that oaks required a summer drought to stay healthy and to check the fungus that might otherwise destroy them. Our local climate, with alternating heavy winter rain and extended summer drought, was good for the oaks. Summer watering was not.

We don't water our oaks on the farm, but once in a while one dies, like the standing oak we made into firewood and the one by the driveway that was still alive but whose weakened roots would no longer hold it upright. We were cautious about walking near the dead tree in the upper woods, especially as it periodically dropped its branches and eventually became a gray snag in the forest. Finally the snag fell over, and Bill spent many summer days cutting it into firewood for winter.

Besides a handful of giants, there are hundreds of smaller oak trees on our place. The trees in our younger oak forests average eight to twelve inches in diameter, and yet they may be sixty years old or more. Though not so terrifying when they fall, these smaller trees also sometimes topple over or simply die standing and fail to leaf out one spring. I know it is part of the climax forest process, and that trees are opportunistic. When they are crowded, get little sunlight, and share nutrition with a large family, their growth can be slow, and some of the trees die off for lack of sun and nutrition. Others, which have been a seemingly fixed size for several years, suddenly take advantage of an opening and put on a growth spurt. In the spring following a year of an especially abundant acorn crop, which seems to happen about every five years, the woods are full of tiny oak trees two or three inches high, but only a few will survive and grow large in the dark understory of the crowded forest.

A forester in eastern Oregon once showed me the rings on a cross section of lodgepole pine that had been growing in a dense forest, now thinned by bark beetle infestation. Though the trunk was small enough for my hands to meet around it, the tree had laid down over eighty rings. I imagined some of the slender oaks in our woodlot must have done the same.

Our oaks are a reminder of the original oak savanna habitat of this valley. Other native plants associated with oak savanna include wild rose, snowberry, poison oak, and indigenous grasses. All of these are on our farm. The oak savanna that flourished in this area for at least seven thousand years was disrupted in our time by cultivated farms and development. In past times, the savanna was maintained by fire, sometimes caused by lightning strikes but also, anthropologists and historical botanists believe, deliberately set by the native Kalapuya Indians in order to maintain the open valley grasslands most favorable to supporting and hunting game animals, such as deer. Isolated oaks, small clusters and forests, with large expanses of native grasslands would have been ideal for this.

When we drive down the valley past highly cultivated farms and pastures, Bill often remarks on the occasional small stand of old oaks in the middle of a wheat field or pasture and wonders aloud why the farmer left the trees. I try to imagine an explanation. If it was ever grazing land, the trees would have provided a protected place for livestock to get out of the weather. The trees may have served as a self-replenishing woodlot when most people burned wood to heat their houses. When Native Americans hereabout set fires to keep the grasslands open, this would have prevented the oaks from spreading, but clusters of big fire resistant oaks would have survived. Sometimes these clusters of aged oaks are near a house where a farmer might have saved them as windbreaks or to provide shade in hot weather. Finally, and this theory I find most sympathetic, I think people must have a natural affinity for trees. Even if their livelihood depended on having cleared land, they would have enjoyed the beauty of some big old trees on the landscape.

The oak forest that lines our pastures is a mere suggestion of oak savanna, but it is also a small part of a much larger oak forest that joins more forest behind our property, and, to the west, an oak forest that stretches all the way to the Coast Range, where, at higher and foggier elevations, oaks eventually give way to maples and Douglas firs.

Not many years ago, a stranger came up our driveway. He told us he had been hired by the county to check on forestland allotments. Part of our property is listed as woodlot or forest, which is taxed at a lower rate than residential property. Trees provide a very slow payoff in the world of farming. A farmer with land in forest may never see a crop in his lifetime, but tax reductions such as this encourage farmers to set aside forestland for future use. This man had checked aerial photographs of our place and decided we didn't have enough trees to qualify. He told us, unless we increased the density of our forestland, we would have to pay back taxes and our annual property taxes would go up. We agreed to add trees, though it seemed as if we had more than enough. He strongly recommended that we put in fir and pine, even though we suggested they would be less true to the original character of the land than oaks. In contradiction, he claimed the oaks were crowding out the natural fir and pine in the valley. That didn't sound right, but we caved to pressure from this supposed expert; Bill ordered eight hundred evergreen seedlings to plant in the fall.

Still, the man's claim that the oaks were crowding out the evergreens didn't seem to make sense. The oaks are so much slower growing and have been around a lot longer in the Willamette Valley. The fir and pine trees are faster growing and more characteristic of the mountains and coast. If anything, it seemed that the fir trees creeping up adjacent to oak forests would shade and overwhelm the oaks.

That same year, as if the oaks were staging a protest, there were an amazing number of acorns. In all our years on the property, I had never seen so many ripe acorns falling from the oaks. This was true not only on our farm. Everywhere we looked we saw that acorns were wildly abundant, including at Champoeg Park and on the Linfield College campus. We could not walk through the woods without crushing dozens of acorns at every step. We collected acorns from underneath the old oaks and spread them on the edges of fields, where we hoped they would sprout.

The coniferous seedlings arrived when the fall rains began, and Bill planted four hundred pines and four hundred firs—the pines in the area below the vineyard and the firs in the top part of the sheep pasture, which Bill had fenced off from the sheep, who would have made quick snacks of the seedlings. The firs were planted in an area in front of our old oak woods. I wondered if these seedlings would grow up and obscure the oaks, but trees grow slowly so there would be time to think about it.

At first, the seedlings seemed to do well, and we felt lucky that we had had a mild winter and a wet spring. Then during the summer heat, many of the firs died, especially during August when the temperature was commonly in the 90s. Aldo Leopold described a similar experience in *A Sand County Almanac.* We felt sad as one fir after another turned rusty red. Evergreens do not make a comeback after they reach that state. My brother-in-law, a state forester, shared a bit of forestry wisdom: "red is dead." He also laughed when we told him the visitor insisted we didn't have enough trees to qualify as woodland. He gestured around at the density of our woodlots. Our place overflows with trees. If anything, he said, we could do some thinning. I could only guess our visitor had been hired to go on a fishing expedition to raise property tax revenue.

We planted the firs on the west side of the property, and they got the full blast of summer's hot afternoons, which must have been hard on them as baby trees. As the weather cooled off, and we had a couple of light rains, it looked as if about one-third of the original planting of firs would make it, and so it has. The pines, meanwhile, did better on the lower, east side of the property. This is perhaps because it is an area with more natural shade, and mainly gets early daylight, or perhaps the pines were better suited to our land than firs. I have read that once upon a time valley pines, related to the ponderosa, were much more abundant in this area than they are now.

The following year, in contrast, the oaks seemed to make almost no acorns, but wherever acorns had fallen the preceding year, hundreds of tiny seedlings sprouted, three-leaved little oak trees about three inches tall. These seedlings were now impossibly dense under the oak woods. In our yard, Bill marked a couple hundred with red, plastic tape. Perhaps we would transplant a few when they went dormant and lost their three leaves later on in the fall. It wouldn't be easy. Oak seedlings put down a much longer root than what they show above ground, so they aren't easy to transplant.

Time has passed, and of the various planted and scattered acorns in various parts of the sheep pasture, only a few seem to have taken root. Either the sheep ate the sprouts or rodents sniffed out the acorns during the long, wet winter. Or perhaps the gophers pulled them underground and ate them there. Looking on the sunny side, perhaps the acorns helped support the beautiful silver-gray squirrels that live in our woods.

In the meantime, something interesting occurred. After the abundance of acorns and other nuts in the fall, and a mild winter, there was a population boom in rodents. We found ourselves fighting the mice that helped themselves to the chicken feed each night. When Bill took the tractor out to mow, mice scattered every which way ahead of him. It was not just on our place either. *The Capital Press,* a statewide farming newspaper, carried stories with complaints about a plague of rodents that year and said that many farmers lost much of their wheat crop due to mice and voles. I would guess that the previous year's abundance of nuts and acorns brought a population surge in the rodent world. The interconnectedness of living things is like a series of waves at the beach, each appearing as an individual and yet resulting in an accumulation of effects. I wondered what called forth the unusual flood of acorns that year and when it might come again.

One more sign of nature's balancing act occurred. After the year of abundant acorns, walnuts, and filberts, and the following seasons of mice and voles, we experienced a year of plentiful raptors. The usual red-tails, kestrels, and northern harriers showed up in greater abundance, and we were treated all winter long to a white-tailed kite, which appeared every morning on the road where we made our routine dog walk. We also saw merlins and Cooper's and sharp-shinned hawks. It must have been good hunting for them that year.

In the meantime, who knew what the coming winter would bring? Whatever happened, the tiny oak seedlings would make a record of it in their rings. Years later, when I hope the world still has room for giant, old trees, maybe one of these seedlings, grown ancient, will fall, and some curious person counting the rings will say, there was the year of this or that, so long ago.

Another oak disaster, or rather, a move to prevent one. Sadly, the big oak by the back door had to come down. The estimate to have the oak felled and cut into sixteen-inch slabs was $1,700. The tree had begun showing a heavy, white fungus between the three joined trunks during the rainy fall. Since its companion tree of the same age and form fell and crushed the three cars, I had been worried about this one, so near the house and looming over the walk from the kitchen door. We made arrangements.

When I came home from work one afternoon it had been felled. I have a hard time describing the feeling of sadness that swept over me at the sight. Losing the beautiful tree was hard enough, but dealing with the mess left behind was overwhelming. The arborists had dropped the three trunks away from the house, and said they would cut the wood into sixteen-inch slabs, turn the smaller pieces into wood chips, grind the stump down with their stump grinder, and finally clean up after themselves. They had done so to a point, but my mind went blank as I tried to move one of the sixteen-inch slabs and realized just how heavy it was. How would we ever transport it, much less split it into usable wood? I had thought they would pile the wood neatly somehow, but the slabs lay across the ground like checker pieces tossed aside from a giant's game, filling the yard and the parking area, with mounds of sawdust piled here and there. I thought about selling the place and moving to a city house with miniature trees and a tiny yard to look after.

The arborists said it would take about two years for the wood to dry enough to be good firewood. Bill had been working so hard on the house, trying to finish remodeling the two guest bedrooms. We had been living in disorder and sawdust from the remodel for more than six weeks. I longed for a return to some sort of order.

It would have been easier to just ignore this tree by our back door, but as my worries about it increased I found I was going in and out of the house with a kind of dread that it would fall suddenly as the other one had, crushing cars, the house, maybe even someone. Now that it was down, I worried about the cost and the mess and anxiety ate away at my love of our poor, old farm. Briefly it felt as if the world was collapsing with the tree.

And yet I am a natural optimist. I still love to walk through our oak woods. Some of the tallest trees have what must be squirrel nests at the tops, structures of sticks and leaves that sway gently, seventy feet or more off the ground. Imagine being a baby squirrel and sleeping in a cradle like that.

The man from the tax assessor's office referred to our oaks as "scrub oaks," and claimed they were not valuable enough to qualify for a forest or woodlot tax rate. When I announced that they were *Querqus garryana*, he wasn't impressed. Later, I looked up the term "scrub oak" and found that it actually refers to a different kind of oak called *Quercus dumosa*, which is said to morph into a variety of other forms of oak. The website I looked at seemed to associate it mainly with California and said that scrub oaks were small, more like shrubs, though some might grow to twelve to twenty feet. I wondered if the name might refer to the miniaturized oaks we had seen in the southern Oregon Siskyous, an ancient landform with anomalous plant varieties, or to some other kind of oak. Scrub oak indeed!

After the tree by the kitchen door was gone, we blocked in a small garden in its place and planted it with shrubs, herbs, and bulbs. It was no substitute for a spreading, ancient oak, but I reminded myself of the words of the arborist, who passed judgment on the strange fungus crawling up its three trunks.

"Well," he said, "It's going to fall down sometime, but I can't tell you when."

Two years passed and another rainy winter arrived. We warmed ourselves with logs chopped from the sixteen-inch-thick oak slabs. There was a great deal of comfort in the heat and the brightness from our woodstove, and I knew the tree, beautiful and splendid as it was, had to go. I might be part-Celt, as my Scots-American father would have insisted, but I was definitely not willing to make human sacrifices to oak trees.

Siena

I got an odd phone call not long after the fall of the great, three-boled oaks. It went like this:

The phone rang. A man's voice asked for me by name, and then said, "Hi, I'm Chuck-something-or-other. Do you know Jim Something-or-other?"

"No," I said.

Chuck-something-or-other told me he worked for my textbook publisher and that Jim-something-or-other, who also worked for our publisher, had told him I had a villa in Siena, Italy.

My mind reeled. Did I? Was it possible? How wonderful.

All week after the big oak fell and crushed the three cars in our driveway, I had been worrying about getting a new car, or at least a good used car. You have to have a reliable car in the country. The insurance company was still deliberating about what to give me for the flattened one. Probably too little to replace it. It was an old car, but it was mine and paid for, and I had faithfully changed its oil every thirty-five hundred miles. It did have dog hair on the upholstery and smelled like the dogs, but otherwise it was a good car. I had planned on driving it for at least three more years. So much for planning. I didn't really have enough money to buy a new car. Besides that, one of the sheep was off her feed, we might need to pay a vet, and we were having some problems with the plumbing. It had been raining for four weeks straight. It was still raining.

"No," I said reluctantly. "I don't think I have a villa in Siena."

"Aren't you the author of…" He named my book.

"Well, yes," I said.

"Jim mentioned you by name. He said you have a villa in Siena."

The possibility that I had a villa in Siena was becoming more real to me by the moment. Perhaps I had been amnesiac. I could use a break. I could sell my villa and buy a new car. Or more exciting, I could move to Siena and give up driving. Stranger things had happened. I considered this, and then, regretfully, conceded it was not likely.

"Really, I don't have a villa in Siena."

"I was hoping to rent it from you," he said, "but if you're sure ..."

"I'm pretty sure."

"Maybe Jim was drinking. Sorry to bother you." He hung up, genuinely disappointed, but no more so than I.

My husband came into the room then. "Who was that?"

I was feeling wistful now. I asked him, "If I had a villa in Siena you'd know about it, wouldn't you?" He regarded me intently, as if I'd been keeping something secret from him. "Do you?"

"I wish that tree hadn't fallen on the car," I said. "And sometimes I wish I had a villa in Siena."

The Dog Diaries

❖

Guy—2000

I was born in Kansas, where my parents raised sheep and had a working border collie named Fanny. I have a small, old picture of Fanny staring into the camera. The picture is brown and faded, but Fanny looks smart and intent as she peers through the mists of time. I consider her my first border collie, already in the house when my parents brought me home from the Abilene hospital that frosty April morning in 1939. I think I was imprinted then with border collies. This doesn't mean I'm good at managing them, just that I love the way they look and think and behave. Though I like dogs in general, no other dog looks as beautiful to me as a border collie.

Jack, the dog I got when we moved to the country in 1987, died suddenly at the age of thirteen. I missed him a lot. When I heard his breeder had a new litter of puppies, I went to look them over and ended up choosing a pup we named Guy. The two dogs were similar in appearance: black and white males, on the large side, with short-haired, smooth, rain-shedding coats. But of course every dog is an individual. Jack was an athlete with an athlete's self-possessed composure. Friendly but not overly-so. Except for the common border collie fear of loud noises, he had an agreeable, calm temperament, and he was a jumper in spades. From a standing start he could fly into the back of our pickup—the tailgate up—without touching his toenails on the edge.

Guy was different. He was more bitey and more incorrigible, and from the beginning he also seemed to need a lot more physical comfort. When he and his littermates were only two weeks old, their mother caught her head in a fence and strangled. I hated to imagine the tiny puppies nearby hearing the sounds of her struggle, then silence, and then the long wait till their people returned home to find what had happened. We accept the fact that emotional distress may have long-lasting effects on human children. How does it affect puppies when they lose their mother this way? After the accident, the breeder hand-fed the pups until they could eat on their own. Then she was eager to find them homes as soon as possible.

I wondered how much Guy's personality was affected by the trauma of his mother's accidental death. Guy was bigger than any border collie I'd had, even bigger than Jack, so I was sure he hadn't suffered food deprivation, probably the opposite, as the owner worked to assure the pups' survival. But even when he was four months and forty pounds, he still wanted to climb up on my lap and cuddle in the evenings. He liked to curl himself into a tight ball of sleek fur, tucking his nose into my waist and falling asleep after a hiccup or two. Whatever the reason, this pup was both affectionate and aggressive. The disciplinary bites and growls of Mollie, our elderly border collie, did little to settle his hash when he was trying to persuade her to romp and nip him in return. A scolding from me elicited defiant yaps instead of shame and compliance.

Books on dog training and behavior, sometimes offering contrary advice, seem to be in endless supply. I wanted to do everything right in training him, so I hauled out my old dog-training books and added some new ones.

I still remember some of the odd tips. One of my books said that while housebreaking a new pup you should never let the dog see you pee in the bathroom, lest he take that as a model. I don't invite my dogs into the bathroom anyway, though once in a while, especially when I am lounging in the tub reading the latest New Yorker, one will push open the door as if to inquire, what's taking so long?

Keeping the bathroom door closed when in use was easy advice to follow, but one day when the door to the empty bathroom was ajar and I noticed Guy looking in with curiosity, I let him go in to investigate. He went to the tub, sniffed the rim delicately, arched his neck and peered over the side. He went to the toilet, sniffed the bowl, peered around it, sniffed the floor, the seat, the back. He went to the scale on the floor, sniffed the scale, touched his nose lightly to the platform of the scale, the side, the floor around it. He went to the sink, looked up, took a deep breath through distended nostrils. Then he stood a moment, filling his nose with all the scents of a bathroom, did one last sniff of the small carpet in front of the sink, turned and saw me watching him, then exited the room, his curiosity, and his nose, apparently satisfied.

A dog's nose is a thousand times more sensitive to smells than a human nose. I still use small dog snacks to play "find the goodies" with the dogs in the house. Their noses lead them from one hiding spot to another. On walks through our country neighborhood, smells are the main source of the dogs' attention. If I visit someone else with a dog, when I return home my dogs thoroughly sniff my shoes, my pants legs, look into my face, sniff some more. They are clearly asking, Who is this dog you've been hanging out with and where are you keeping him? When I hide a toy out of sight in the living room and then call Guy into the room, he visibly homes in on a trail of chew-toy-scented air. I wished I could do this trick when I misplace my car keys or reading glasses.

In any case, as best I could, when Guy came into our household I worked at basic training, took him to a simple obedience class where he could mingle with other dogs and learn a few basic rules, and enjoyed getting to know him.

Guy—2004

Our dogs are mainly companions, but I'd often imagined what it would be like to train a herding dog. I'd heard a lot of stories about Fanny and the other working dogs from my parents' Kansas days. When Guy was four years old, I called a border collie trainer about taking herding lessons and asked about training at his age, which she said was fine. He was always interested in our sheep and stared intently at them through the fence when I took him to the barn to feed them and put them in at night. I wondered how he would do in a class.

I knew Guy usually considered himself in charge. When I threw a ball, instead of returning it nicely he liked to tease me by twisting his head back and forth, keeping the ball just out of my reach. A major border collie talent is anticipation; they love to stay one step ahead of the game. I couldn't help laughing when he acted so pig-headed and that just encouraged his bossy behavior. I often ended up on the ground wrestling him for it. Not good discipline.

The breeder I got him from was an excellent trainer. Her dogs followed her like a school of fish. Eyes locked on, they tracked whatever she was doing and swayed with her commands and wishes—this way, that way. How did she do that?

I asked her how she trained her dogs.

"Basically I just talk to them," she said.

In the obedience class we took when Guy was a year old he did a good job with heel, stop, sit, come, and so on, but everything was keyed to treats. Guy had a voracious appetite and would do just about anything for food.

I'd read a couple of books on training herding dogs and watched videos, but it wasn't easy to translate the moves and corrections into actual practice. I wasn't even sure I actually understood the term "correction" when applied to dog training. Correction came up a lot. Did it mean punishment, reinforcement, alternative moves? I'd gone to dog trials and was fascinated with the way handlers of herding dogs were able to get their dogs to work on command: come by (circle clockwise); away to me (circle counter clockwise); lie down; asking the dog to move up or separate one or more sheep from the rest of the flock; penning; and the final command, that'll do, which signaled the end of working. A skilled dog handler could do this with just whistles, gestures, seemingly effortless voice commands, even body language, and at great distances. But how on earth did they get to this point?

Would I be able to learn how to actually work with him? Until now, he had mostly gotten his own way. I knew we needed firsthand experience, guided by an expert. Guy and I signed up for a class.

I woke early on the first day of the ten-week herding class, scheduled for 9 a.m. on Saturdays. I wasn't sure how long it would take me to find the place on a country road somewhere between Oregon City and Mulino. Guy was excited as I was, and stood up the whole way, panting and looking excitedly out of one side of the car and then the other. He loved riding in any vehicle. Go fast is the border collie motto, even when someone else is driving.

It was a cool morning, the second day of fall, and though the weather was bright and dry it definitely had an autumn feeling. There was a floating mist over some of the low-lying fields and bright sun above as I drove past the vineyards and hazelnut orchards on the way to Newberg. Ash trees had started turning yellow and brown on the creek bottoms, and wherever there were maples and other deciduous trees, I saw touches of red and gold in the top leaves.

Guy and I arrived fifteen minutes early. To make sure I had the right place, I pulled over on the country road to look at the printed directions. A small, gray-haired woman in boots and coveralls over a warm shirt stepped out of a nearby driveway and waved.

"Are you Barbara?" she asked, and gestured toward the drive. "I'm Kathy. Just park right here."

She filled me in on the routine for what she called "going potty" away from the area where we'd be working, Guy going potty that is. The training field was a small, sloped pasture, where a dozen cross-breed sheep, most of them hair sheep, stood watching us. They looked very different from our Romneys, which had been bred for the long wool that Bill handspun and wove into soft blankets. When I asked why she'd chosen them, Kathy said she wasn't interested in wool. Hair sheep have a coarse, hairy coat that doesn't need to be sheared. They are shedding animals, and their fleece sheds or peels off periodically.

Hair sheep are also often referred to as meat sheep, since this is their main use as livestock, but according to Kathy these sheep lived to be herded. I noticed that when they moved they were more like a coordinated ballet troupe than our Romneys. They kept a tight group, their clean heads all turning the same way at once, just as they ran the same way, shoulders almost touching. Our sheep didn't cluster like that—when they went out in the field they scattered all over, and even though they flocked together part of the time, mainly when they were lying down to ruminate or going into the barn at night, they often took off in different directions when startled or when Guy tried to make them move. I wondered if Kathy's sheep behaved this way because of their breed or whether they had just been trained by having been worked by dogs so much. The training books talked about sheep that were "dog broke," meaning they were used to being worked or herded. Hers were obviously dog broke.

As the class began, Kathy told us: "Your dog needs to remember who buys the dog food." Suddenly I realized that Guy wasn't the only one being trained here. Kathy also made it clear that she was scornful of dependence on treats for training. A border collie is supposed to naturally love herding, to do it for the love of it, and to satisfy a need that verges on obsession. Even at the beginning, trainers weigh the likelihood of a dog being a good herder by its "showing interest." In sheep, not dog biscuits.

Historically, the dog's instinct to herd was based on capturing and killing for food. Domesticated dogs were selected for their hunting abilities and put in the service of human beings. Nowadays, of course, a dog that chases sheep on its own is a disaster, but it's still all connected: hunting, prey, joy, instinct, the need to control, and, when things go right, the need to please the handler.

I filled out the consent papers, which relieved Kathy of liability for personal injuries, falls, and so on, and promised, on my part, to pay for any sheep maliciously injured by my dog. I looked over the other material she handed me, the summary of her training methods and her formula for training, what she called the four F's: Fast, Fair, Firm, Forgive. I hoped the last applied to me as well as to my dog. Soon two other women and their dogs arrived for class, and we introduced ourselves. Guy play-bowed to Hilary's dog, Hester, a pretty, brown crossbreed. Laura had brought Fisher. As nearly as we could figure out, Fisher was Guy's nephew. Our dogs came from the same breeder, and so the dogs' relationship was not too much of a coincidence since that breeder knew and had recommended Kathy.

No doubt a lot of border collies are related if you look back far enough, though it might be hard to tell for certain. Breeding papers list only four generations back, and dog generations come around pretty quickly. And yet working dogs are not apt to be as inbred as show breeds. Working dogs have been chosen for performance rather than inbred for conformation to a uniform appearance or style. Border collie breeders in America also make a practice of importing dogs now and then from the UK. This is done to incorporate choice breeding lines and to maintain diversity. That healthy diversity manifests itself in a wide range in size, coat, and overall appearance in border collies. Most of them are black and white, but they can also be red and white, sable, or a heathered sort of blue-gray or reddish gray mix, known as merle. Some have a smooth, short coat, others have thick long hair, and adult dogs differ in sizes from around thirty-five pounds to sixty or more.

Fisher was a slender black and white dog with large, erect ears and a smooth coat. He was about two years old, and had gone through a previous class with Kathy. He stood behind Laura, tense with excitement. Gradually he settled and began to focus on the sheep on the other side of the field. Obviously Fisher was "showing interest."

I guessed that the two young women in the class were in their thirties. I was sixty-five when I started taking herding classes. I wondered if I would be agile enough and have the endurance needed to get out there and run up and down the field. I'd had experience with being knocked off my feet by running sheep, and I didn't want that to happen again—even a relatively small sheep determined to escape a tense situation can knee-cap you. I also didn't want to slip and fall in the sloped, muddy pasture.

To begin, Kathy had us walk around with our dogs in the field. She noticed how Guy pulled on the leash and said that meant he was "abusing" me. Strong language. She said that he was putting himself in charge and shouldn't be able to do that. I'd been working on his heel and thought I'd made some progress, but in the excitement of getting out there with the sheep, dogs, and strange people, he was ignoring me entirely. She took the leash and showed me a couple of maneuvers to get him to heel. She also explained that her definition of heel wasn't the obedience class sort of heel—it just meant the dog was supposed to be behind you, one side or the other, and attuned to your moves.

The first correction she showed me was a quick military-style turn to the left, or right, depending on which side the dog was coming up on. She took Guy's leash from me and began to walk. At the moment of turning she put her knee up, and Guy ran right into it. She wasn't kicking or hitting him, just creating an irritating obstacle. After she did this several times, he dropped back and stopped trying to get past her when they walked. The other move utilized the long slender herding wand. With Guy on one side, she flicked the wand back and forth, as if it were the pendulum of a clock, in front of her body as she walked, When Guy started to move ahead, he inevitably ran into the wand.

Kathy returned the leash. "You aren't hitting him," she said. "The stick is there, and if he decides to walk ahead and run into it, that's his doing. And he won't like it, you'll see." He didn't, and by practicing those two moves it seemed that he and I both made some small progress. Kathy also wanted to stop Guy from moving through the gate into the field before me. She showed me how with Vic, her own young dog that was well trained but not yet perfect. "When the dog starts to run ahead through the gate, bang it shut on him. He won't like that, and he'll hold back." Sure enough, she started into the pen with Vic, and at one point he surged ahead of her. She banged the door on his nose, not hard enough to hurt him but hard enough to be annoying. He jumped back, and the next time they went through the gate he waited for her.

After these exercises, which felt demanding to me, she said that we all needed to see what it took to move the sheep in a controlled manner. She asked us to go one at a time into the pasture without our dogs and try to round up the sheep ourselves, basically to move them from a corner where they liked to hide out, to a standing place under a tree on the opposite corner of the pasture. We would be the dogs, while the dogs watched from the sidelines. I wondered how Guy would like that. Probably not much.

Sheep point their heads in the direction they're going to run, and we were supposed to read their intentions from that. I thought I was moving them along okay, walking up on them, stopping, and then running around them to get them going. But every time I thought I had them in place, they would suddenly break free and run back into their comfortable corner. I tried this for a while, and then I called out, "I can't run as fast as a dog or a sheep!"

"You're right," said Kathy, laughing. "But now you know what it takes to move those sheep."

The final exercise involved going in with our dogs on leash, one at a time, and trying to move the sheep. Guy was oddly distracted. At home he focused on the sheep, but here he was sometimes looking at the sheep, sometimes looking at me, and sometimes looking toward the other people and dogs where they sat on the porch of the small trailer house, which was Kathy's work station. He was apparently trying to figure out what we were doing there, and so was I.

The rain had quit early in the morning, and the day was now hot. Guy took a long drink from the water bucket. Then, after a few minutes of excitedly watching Hilary and Hester, he returned to the bucket where he again lapped slowly and luxuriously.

About that time, Laura's mother showed up. Laura said she had been enthusing to her parents over the past year, as she worked first with her old dog, Kvai, and now with young Fisher, but neither of her folks had seen the lessons firsthand. Now Laura's dog Fisher did some work off leash, bringing the sheep around and to her, though a few times he refused to stop when she told him to. I thought he was remarkable, but Laura seemed a little frustrated when Fisher didn't show off his best skills in front of her mother. I knew the feeling. One's own pride gets tangled with the dog.

I wondered if I would ever get Guy to respond like Fisher and resolved to get a professional shepherd's wand and a whistle to practice at home. The herding wand is an essential tool. The handler uses it to indicate direction or to apply pressure to the dog (not by contact but by gesture), and sometimes to shoo the sheep one way or another. We were using Kathy's lightweight fiberglass sticks as wands, but now I wanted one of the fancy, tapered, graphite models, which would be longer, sturdier, have a comfortable, braided handgrip, and which might even serve as a kind of balancing stick for me in the slippery mud. Besides, I liked the magical sound of having my own "wand."

Over the Saturdays that followed, I did my best to apply Kathy's instructions, and Guy learned to get around the sheep, to move up or stop when I wanted him to, and to generally behave himself on the field. But I could never really get him to do a fast outrun, the move in which the dog, at high speed, runs a wide, flanking curve around the sheep in order to place himself in the balance point, on the opposite side of the flock, preparatory to bringing them to the handler. He wasn't a jumper, and as it turned out he wasn't a high-speed runner either. Instead, Guy liked to go partway around at a leisurely pace, stopping short, and then start driving.

Driving is where the dog walks the sheep forward to some preferred destination. It's important in moving the sheep into a different field or barn and essential when large flocks need to be driven across big open spaces, but it's not the same as doing a stylish outrun and bringing them to the handler. Occasionally, Guy would drive the sheep toward me, but never with the dogged steadiness with which he simply got behind them and walked them to a corner of the field or a fence line.

Sometimes dogs get the sheep revved up so they cluster and start to run wildly, in which case the handler needs to slow the dog down to get things under control. Guy was quite the opposite and seemed to have a soporific effect on the sheep. Once he got them moving, they would simply walk slowly and purposefully in the direction he'd started them. He didn't nip at their heels or try to get them moving faster, and they didn't seem at all alarmed. In fact, they seemed almost hypnotized. He just walked them in a line as if they were in a trance till they were someplace he could park them: at a fence, a corner, or a closed gate. Then he would look back at me as if to ask, are you satisfied?

Guy—2013

There was one thing that troubled me during herding classes with Guy: he started to show a dark side. Kathy emphasized being "the boss" with your dog. One day when she got close to him and looked down he growled. This happened when he was tied to the fence and couldn't get away. Her comment was, "You need to be careful with him." As he got older, I noticed that if he was penned, cornered, in the back of the truck, or otherwise confined, and felt confronted, he showed his teeth and sometimes growled or barked at anyone entering his space. With small children he sometimes ran tight, herding circles around them to bring them under his control. Needless to say, this frustrated and frightened them. As he grew older this behavior was more troubling, and I began keeping him away from visitors, especially children. A stranger seeming to invade his space was in danger of a sudden bark and snap. I couldn't let a gas station attendant offer him a friendly dog biscuit. If he was riding with me in the car, I always loaded my own groceries.

On the one hand, he was an affectionate dog who loved attention and petting. When I got down on the floor with him, he would throw himself on my lap and roll on his back in a posture equated with submission. He has always wanted to get close to me. When I sit down he still likes to lean against my knees and tuck his head under one of my armpits, his eyes closed in bliss, as I scratch his back. But if something frightens him, or if he is confined and someone approaches, he braces his legs and gets a defensive look in his eye. Throughout the years he has become more and more afraid of loud noises, especially thunder, gunshots, and Fourth-of-July explosions. At the summer's end, when nearby vineyards run their blasted grape cannons to scare off marauding birds, he is a nervous wreck. He even bit me once during a lightning storm when a blast of thunder sent him in a frenzied scrambling under my desk, and I reached to restrain him.

Since then I have read that the main reason border collies end up in border collie rescue or shelters is a tendency to nip. Normally border collies don't nip their sheep, or people, but it is a fall-back tactic for herding dogs when things feel out of control. Moreover, something whizzing past the dog's head—a scarf, a branch, a toy, a running child, may be a cue for snapping, as the movement awakens the deeply bred instinct to keep anything from getting away. It's a defensive or protective move, not the same as a dog attacking or starting a fight, but it can do damage.

I've had several border collies. Most of them have been unnerved by loud noises and are fairly high strung, but Guy is the only one who has shown a tendency to nip. I wonder about the effects of losing his mother. There is a stage in pup development when the mother dog will discipline bitey pups with a nip of her own or by pinning them to ground. Because Guy's mother died when the pups were only two weeks old, he missed that stage when his mother would have nipped back at any growing pups who were getting too rough with their teeth or who challenged her authority. When our vet checked Guy for behavior cues, she said his snapping behavior was reactive. She added, "Border collies are naturally anxious dogs." Out in the world, on a leash or occasionally running loose at the beach, he normally ignores other dogs and people, and when visitors arrive he is all wag and tail. But in a situation where something startles or frightens him, especially if he is somehow cornered or restrained, we can't trust him not to respond to a perceived threat with a snap.

I brought Guy home when he was barely six weeks old, and he has always been treated well, so I can only think that something in his nature along with the fact that he missed that developmental stage with his mother have made him the dog he is. I've never had a snappy dog before, and it makes me sad that I have to protect others from him, and even more that I have to protect him from himself. But in the space and privacy of the country, it's not too hard to manage. I love my old dog, and I don't ever want him to get in trouble.

I took my first sheep-herding class with Guy nine years ago. Now he is thirteen years old and showing more white on the muzzle. His hearing is poor, and he needs help to get into the back of the pickup. Guy sometimes runs for short bursts, but he still would rather walk. When he does run, there is a heavy galumphing quality to his gait. Back when we took those first classes he would sometimes run, but he showed his driving temperament early.

Later, when I was taking classes with my younger dog, Maggie, Kathy would sometimes recall Guy as a dog with a great talent for driving. I wasn't sure whether she was just trying to make me feel better about the fact that he was never speedy on the playing field or if it was a true compliment. I like to think the latter, since Kathy was a frank and upfront kind of woman. But even though I could never get him to do a high-speed outrun, Guy's driving skills have turned out to be somewhat useful at home, say, if the chickens are into my flowers and start kicking things up. Then I roust Guy and say, "Put the chickens back." He stirs his aging bones, gets behind them, and the chickens start moving. Now and then, as he walks them back to their pen, he glances my way to make sure he's doing the right thing. When they are on the other side of the fence, he looks at me once more as if to say, will that do?

Thank you, dear old dog. Yes, that'll do. He wags his tail and smiles a tongue-out, doggy smile.

Maggie—2005

Our younger border collie, Maggie, has a more traditional appearance than Guy's. She is a dainty eater, full grown at forty pounds, and has a black-and-white, thick, long or "rough" coat. She looks more like our old dog Mollie. Our sweet, elderly border collie Mollie was still around when Guy was a pup but died suddenly at the age of sixteen. Mollie was the dog that always slept next to my side of the bed, the one I had to be careful not to step on if I got up in the dark, the one who followed me to the kitchen when I went out to make coffee. I missed her, and having only one dog felt off-balance somehow, but I waited a couple of years until I saw a picture of border collie pups on the notice board at the veterinarian's office. I went to see them and inevitably fell for a pup the breeders called Princess. Though we renamed her Maggie, I sometimes imagined she still thought of herself as a princess. Our dogs are an integral part of the family, so getting a new one was a big deal. When we went to pick her up the week before Christmas, Eben and Delphi, two of the grandkids, were visiting. They volunteered to hold the pup on the way home, but she seemed panicked about the car ride so I tucked her under my coat and held her on my lap. We almost made it home before she barfed her tummy-full of dry dog food. The kids were glad she was on my lap, not theirs. Maggie has come a long way since then and has never again been sick in the car, but she doesn't enjoy car trips the way Guy does. He just needs to hear the words "car" or "truck" before he's at the appropriate vehicle door wagging his tail. When Maggie realizes we're going for a drive, she holds back at the car door and feints one way and then another. At the last moment, when she figures I'm not going to let her off the hook, she gathers herself and makes a flying leap into the vehicle where she crouches in the seat as low as possible. Dogs really do have innately different personalities. Otherwise, Maggie is easygoing, playful, and relaxed. I don't have to worry about her nipping grandchildren. And yet, with Guy I saw a side of her that doesn't show up in any other situation. I don't remember what he was doing exactly, checking out her food dish or bumping into her when they were chasing a ball, but she went ballistic. Her lips curled back, and her teeth went on display. She snarled and grabbed his cheek in her teeth. It was like someone grabbing an unruly kid's collar and giving him a shake. It looked odd since the first time this happened she was half his size. She still reprimands him if they are romping and he gets too rough or too wild about something, circling and barking at the vacuum cleaner for instance. Occasionally and inappropriately, she "disciplines" Guy if I scold her for something, as if she considers herself beyond reproach and anything wrong must be his fault. A princess is never wrong, and Guy never retaliates. Instead he backs off with a humble air, as if saying, I beg your pardon your highness. I described this to an acquaintance, who is a psychologist and a dog behavior expert, and her only comment was, "Sometimes it takes a good bitch to get a male dog in line." I wondered if Guy was now getting the straightening out he had missed when he lost his mother.

When Maggie was a year and a half old, I decided to try her on sheep. Perhaps, I thought, by starting her out young we could accomplish wonders.

It was still dark out the morning of her first herding class. I was prepared for mud, wearing rain pants, my red rain jacket, and brand new muck boots. Daylight savings time had come to an end, and months of sunshine had turned suddenly to clouds and rain.

It was exciting to think of what I might accomplish with a young dog, but I was afraid Maggie would be too spooked by the car ride to be interested in sheep. How wrong I was. She tucked down in the car, but the moment we arrived her stare was fixed on the dozen or so sheep in Kathy's pasture. On Saturday mornings thereafter she was eager for the ride.

I'd heard Kathy say that every novice trainer with a new dog swears they will not make whatever mistakes they made with the previous one, and the thought crossed my mind. I don't know if I made specific mistakes with Guy, but there were things I could never teach him to do as well as I would have liked. I was determined to do a better job with Maggie.

Of course, Maggie had already formed some habits, and they weren't all good. For one thing, she was such a lithe and agile little dog that she could easily slip through the fence and into our sheep pasture. Occasionally she was inspired to check out the sheep on her own. If she was here one minute and gone the next, the pasture was where to look. Our own geriatric sheep had had a couple of bad experiences with stray dogs, but they knew Maggie. If she approached them they made their way behind a bush or into a stand of oaks and stood there, refusing to move as she stared and did her best to give them "the eye," that instinctive, focused stare a border collie uses to control livestock. I sent her to the house if she tried this stunt.

Since Kathy's sheep were dog broke, they didn't panic when dogs appeared on the scene. Correctly herded, they usually just sailed around the field like a flock of starlings, following one another's cues and most of the time sticking close together. To the sheep, the handler represented safety, and when they felt pressure they tended to follow the person out there directing the dog. This helped in setting up a successful run. If you are training a dog and the sheep come to you for protection, while the dog walks up slowly and calmly from behind, the dog begins to get a feeling for cooperative herding. Then you've actually accomplished quite a lot.

Everyone had been busy since the last class I attended. Kathy had traveled to Scotland the month before, visiting dog owners and attending sheep trials, and she was full of excitement about that. She showed us her scrapbook from the trip. There were pictures of sheep and sheep and more sheep, as well as souvenir pamphlets and pictures from a tour of Edinburgh. Laura had just come back from attending a slow-food movement conference in Turin. She and her partner operated a farm and were active in the Community Supported Agriculture movement. They grew and sold vegetables and fruits to Portland farm subscribers, who wanted local, organic vegetables. Now they were looking for a large piece of rural land to expand their business. Hilary, the owner of Hester, worked as an aide for an Oregon congressman. It was fun to be out in the mud and rain again with our dogs.

The class with Maggie took the same pattern as the one with Guy. This time there were four teams in the class, though the fourth, a young man and his dog, wouldn't be there till the next weekend. The class was supposed to run for three hours, but sometimes went over. We each took about ten to fifteen minutes with the sheep, usually getting three turns each. There were breaks to discuss the lessons and to give the sheep a rest.

The others went first today, and I spent my time trying to convince novice Maggie not to yelp, bark, whine, and squirm when the other dogs were working the sheep. Kathy told me to use a slip chain to give her a correction in the form of a sideways jerk when she started yelping. "Don't drag on her," she said, "just a fast yank to get her attention." It was difficult for me to be stern with Maggie. She wanted to be in with the sheep, and I sympathized, but after a few corrections she settled down to watch quietly instead of embarrassing me by throwing a tantrum.

Fisher was back and showed his skill and experience as Laura sent him on an outrun. He gave a nice wide flank. Then Hilary took a turn with Hester. Not a border collie, Hester had spent her early sessions learning to calm down and pay attention to Hilary's commands. She was large but puppy-like, and in the beginning, when she was starting on sheep, she would sometimes just chase them. Hester was having fun, but the sheep were running every which way, crashing and rolling over, or even jumping a fence to get away. Chasing and herding are not the same thing.

I saw that Hester had made great progress since then. She was more collected. Hilary no longer had to resort to the long drag line to pull her back if she got out of control. Hester was working offline now and paid attention to Hilary's commands of stop and stay and come. It was brilliant progress, especially with a dog not bred for instinctive herding.

Now it was my turn. I was a little nervous. Maggie was my darling baby dog. I wanted her to do well, and I also didn't want to scare her or make her lose enthusiasm. She was supposed to work with me, and I was supposed to be in charge. She needed to know that, but herding dogs also needed to love herding. Would she?

Learning to work your dog is like this. The dog is the dog. You are the trainer or handler. But during classes with Kathy, she was the trainer, and it seemed I was the dog. She was training the handler, more than the dog. If I did something lame in the field with my dog or let her get away with something, I knew Kathy would once again resort to her pointed question, "Who buys the dog food, Barbara?" I never wanted to hear that, nor did I want to be pulled off the field any more than Maggie did. Getting out there with my dog was too much fun.

I took Maggie into the sloped field. Midway up the hill there was an oak tree, which served as a marker and a possible goal for moving sheep. Farther up there was a little, decorative wishing-well sort of thingamajig. It sat there as an obstacle we used to move the sheep around. Sometimes they chose to congregate there as an opening move, but today they had decided to collect in a small stand of oaks in the bottom far corner. No doubt the sheep felt the trees created a safety barrier and complicated things for the dog since there wasn't much room to get behind them in the space between the trees and the fence line.

Kathy asked me to keep Maggie on her lead for the first time out. She wanted me to walk around the sheep with Maggie on the outside, heeling, in the path that she should normally follow on an outrun. I watched my step as I walked down the pasture, slippery with mud and dotted with small rocks protruding through wet grass. A couple of times in the past I'd done the muddy splits.

As we got closer to the sheep they moved uphill and re-gathered in the opposite top corner of the pasture. Calling from the sidelines, Kathy told me to down my dog and put myself uphill between her and the sheep. Maggie lay down and seemed willing to wait as I walked uphill toward the sheep, hoping they would also stay put, at least momentarily. Kathy said placing yourself between the dog and sheep sends a message to the dog about who is in charge. I wasn't sure I was in charge, but I hoped I was giving that impression. By the time I had stopped in front of the sheep and turned, Maggie had begun to creep up the field. I was about to tell her to lie down when Kathy called for me to let her go, so I made the whispered *shsh* noise Kathy told us to use, to start the dog on an outrun. Maggie looked at me with a questioning look and then started running past me and straight at the sheep.

"Down your dog!" Kathy yelled from the sidelines. An out-curving run around the sheep was what we were aiming for and this wasn't it.

Shouting "lie down" as forcefully as I could, I stepped in front of Maggie, but she dodged around me and sheep scattered, running all the way back down the hill and into the grove of small oaks. I yelled a second time and Maggie dropped to her belly, all the while following the sheep with her eyes. Back to square one. I knew from the lessons with Guy that being able to get a good down is a primary way of controlling your dog, so I had practiced with Maggie. At least it worked the second time.

We spent the rest of the morning walking around the sheep and working on "lie down" and "that'll do," the latter being a call for the dog to quit working, come back to the trainer, and get off the field. Over and over I went through the process of setting Maggie up for a run, starting her, pushing her to keep her distance from the flock, and then calling her off when she quit paying attention. If she ignored me and tried to run after the sheep on her own, or dived at a galloping sheep's rear and did what Kathy called "flossing her teeth," the immediate consequence was a firm "that'll do" and our turn ended.

More than once, Kathy told us, "Getting to herd is a reward for a herding dog. You don't reward bad behavior." When she didn't co-operate, Maggie had to sit outside the pasture fence watching others have all the fun. Slowly she seemed to be getting the point.

All in all the first day wasn't bad, but it wasn't until a later class that I made real progress with Maggie. She was responding to "lie down" and "that'll do," and she definitely responded to the *shsh* that told her to circle around the sheep, but the farther she got from me the more her "outruns" tended to veer close to the sheep, not nearly "out" enough. She also wanted to pick her own direction. When I asked for an outrun, she preferred "away to me," circling counter-clockwise. When I tried to get her to run clockwise she would sometimes cross between me and the sheep, instead of cir-cling behind me, which effectively put her in charge and took me out of the partnership.

Kathy told me that dogs can have a preference for either "come by" or "away to me," but Maggie needed to learn to follow my di-rection. By stepping out to block her and make her move the way I wanted, I was getting some results, but it required my running al-most as much as she did. This was exhausting to say the least. Kathy suggested I use my nice mail-order herding stick with the fancy handle more effectively. A herding dog is sensitive to body language and using a herding stick or wand to indicate direction and to apply pressure from a distance is an extension of body language. I realized that half the time I was just waving my stick around, sometimes smacking it on the ground for emphasis but not really using it effectively. Ideally, pointing the wand behind the dog should cause her to speed up in the direction she's going, pointing it at her shoulder would push her to broaden her outrun, and pointing it in front of her head could cause her to slow down or reverse direction, all from a fair distance.

I resolved to be more conscious of where I was pointing or gesturing. It wasn't just a question of calling out commands. I needed to use my body language and my herding stick to connect with, direct, and support my dog. Maggie had the talent and instinct to herd, but she wanted to do it her way and wasn't sure I knew what I was doing. I gathered my resolve, trying to get into a frame of mind that put me in charge and yet also let the dog know that we were working together.

Now the sheep were gathered at a distance, at the top of the field. I walked Maggie downhill, even farther away from the sheep, and told her to lie down. I took her gently by the collar, lifting and turning her so she was facing to the right, in a "come by" direction, not her favorite. I then retraced my steps, putting myself between her and the sheep. I extended my arm and the wand, pointing just behind Maggie, and whispered shsh so she would start moving. It was what she had been waiting for. As if she felt the pressure of my gesture, this time she began to move in a curving line to my right, while I stood pivoting in place, my extended left arm holding the wand and figuratively "pushing" Maggie. The sheep too began to move and soon dog and sheep were traveling in an arc, Maggie just a tad farther out than the sheep, keeping them in orbit around me. It felt amazing.

Kathy called out for me to change directions, and this time I extended my arm and the stick as if to block Maggie on the right so she would turn and run to my left. It worked. It really worked. In a few moments, when I again indicated a change of direction, I was delighted to find that worked too. The others watching from the sidelines suddenly whooped and clapped their hands. It felt great.

Now Maggie was more confident about what I was asking for, and she was willing to cooperate. Using the herding wand was a way to enforce the "away to me" and "come by" commands; it was a tool to help the dog understand what I wanted. Despite his lovely driving, I had never been able to get Guy to do an outrun like this. As my "magic wand" directed Maggie this way and that, it felt as if we were connected by an invisible force. She clearly wanted to work, and she had a lot more natural talent for it than I did. When I was ambiguous or sloppy, she did her best, but she got impatient and took off on her own. We needed to communicate. In a few minutes, Kathy called us off the field. Both the sheep and Maggie were getting tired, and a young dog learning something new needs a chance to absorb what's going on.

It felt great and it felt like progress, but now what? Running the sheep in circles like a wooly merry-go-round was not the point. This was supposed to be herding, not ballet or straight-out sheep harassment. It was time to move on to the next step.

The next time I sent Maggie on an outrun, Kathy told me to give her a down command when she reached what I thought was the balance point, more or less halfway around the sheep. Then, when Maggie stopped, Kathy told me to walk backwards away from the sheep. The idea was to encourage the sheep to walk away from the dog and toward me, their safety zone. Again Kathy had told me to leave the leash on Maggie, to make it easier in case I needed it to catch her, but for the moment at least Maggie sank to the ground and stayed put, keeping her eye on the sheep who were now actually, gratifyingly, walking my way. As the sheep moved closer to me and farther from Maggie, she stood again and moved slowly behind them in a border collie walking crouch. When she got too close and the sheep seemed about to scatter, I downed her again, then let her get up and continue to walk the sheep toward me. As the sheep arrived at my feet, Maggie stood close on the other side of them, totally focused.

"Walk through the sheep," Kathy called out. I did, and the small flock parted calmly. "Now give her a that'll do and take your dog off the field." This time Maggie didn't resist but followed me through the gate, a proper ending to a good workout.

This exercise helped both Maggie and me to understand the importance of finding the balance point. Herding was not circling endlessly, but rather the dog doing an outrun and finding a point from which she could control and move the sheep as needed. The concept of the balance point was not as easy to understand as it might seem. At first when Kathy spoke about moving a dog to the balance point, I pictured a perfect circular geometric figure, sheep in the center, and the figure bisected by a precise line connecting the dog on one side and me on the other. This is approximate, but the balance point is not a stationary pose. Sometimes sheep need to be held in place, but they also need to be moved, sometimes across large distances. Even a small flock of sheep is a fluid entity. Imagine putting pressure on anything pliable or liquid. Too much pressure in the wrong place and the contents will squeeze out one way or another. The balance point is where dog and shepherd have the sheep under control, not squeezing out anywhere. This is good for the sheep too, as they understand falling in line can be a calm, predictable process. Whether the aim is to hold the sheep in place, bring them to the shepherd, or move them somewhere else, the balance point is where dog and handler are positioned as a team to make that happen.

I had to learn to know what I wanted. Maggie had to learn to pay attention to what I was asking from her, as well as using her own instinctive, rambunctious nature.

After our final turn of that day, I gave Maggie a "that'll do." This was the signal for her to take her attention away from the sheep and come to me, preparing to leave the field. I thought we were fine, but as I walked toward the gate the sheep suddenly galloped off in a different direction, and Maggie ran after them. I called, "That'll do!" She hesitated, looked at the sheep, looked at me, took a step toward the sheep, stood still while doing her best to ignore me. "THAT'LL DO!" I shouted again. This time she paused as if trying to make a weighty decision. Sheep? Barbara? Sheep? Barbara? Then she turned and followed me out of the pasture gate.

I should admit, even as she walked off the field, her bright eyes still followed the sheep, clustered at the top of the field now. I was reminded of when granddaughter Delphi visited recently. Delphi stared at Maggie for a moment and then she said, "Her eyes are like coins." I asked her to repeat herself, because I didn't understand what she meant. "Her eyes are like coins," she said again. Then I realized, earlier Delphi had been playing with a pile of bright pennies, and they indeed had the shine of Maggie's bright copper-colored eyes.

When we returned home after that class, Guy studied both of us closely. As I had been preparing to leave earlier that morning, he seemed to be reading my mind. He heeled perfectly, following me to the kitchen, to the bedroom, the laundry room, tight as a burr. He saw me pull out my rain gear, the herding stick, and Maggie's leash. When I went to the car he stood in the driveway until I let Maggie in without inviting him. Then he turned with a sulky look and withdrew into the bushes by the back door. Sometimes border collies are so smart they get their feelings hurt.

Now on our return, he and Bill greeted us. Maggie, normally a light eater who seldom wanted anything midday, went to her dish and barked for food so Bill gave her an extra cup of kibble, which she ate quickly.

While I told Bill about the class, Guy was getting the story of our day in sniffs. No doubt there was plenty to sniff. My clothes were spattered with mud and a little sheep poop as well. I stripped off my rain pants and jacket, then the rest of my clothes. By the time I was out of the shower, Maggie was stretched out on my office couch, which is officially "the dog couch."

I could tell from the way she had flattened herself into unconsciousness that she was totally bushed from her day of herding. Her rain-soaked, shaggy black hair had dried, and her white paws were extended, as if she were making a run, but she slept the deep sleep of a good day's workout. As I watched her, she rolled onto her back, eyes still closed, and threw one paw over her face to shut out the world.

I studied her pointed nose with its white blaze, the half-mast ears soft with velvety black fur, the luxurious white ruff around her neck, and the plumy tail she wrapped around herself. It almost made me wish we humans had furry tails to flaunt. I was tempted to go over and sniff her rain-washed head—but I let her sleep uninterrupted, as she deserved. I went to my favorite couch in the sunroom. Soon, I was snoozing as well. What a good day it had been.

Saturday car rides became something to look forward to. When the class was over, Maggie would leap into the back seat, throw herself down on her blanket, and doze all the way home.

Maggie and I took many classes over several years, sometimes taking a break for a season or two. She would learn to move the sheep and to hold them to me. She would learn to leave the field when asked, though this was the hardest thing of all. She would have been happy to work every day of her life. I knew I wasn't as good a trainer as she was a working dog. I had to go to a different sort of work all week—but we had many wonderful Saturday classes out in the field. I was just happy to have fulfilled a lifetime dream, stirred in me by my father's stories about long-ago days in Kansas, when the family raised sheep and had a border collie named Fanny.

Afterthoughts—2014

I still have my beautiful, black-and-white dogs but haven't taken a class for a while. I heard from Kathy that she and her husband had retired, sold their farm, and moved to another state to be closer to grandchildren. I do miss those Saturdays. Though it took me an hour each way to go to and from Kathy's place, I didn't mind at all. The drive itself was a delight. I loved looking at the farms and horses, the peach and hazelnut orchards, the varied trees and the plant nurseries. I crossed some form of flowing water every few miles: Milk Creek, the Pudding River, the Tualatin, Champoeg Creek, and the countless trickles and nameless streams that passed through culverts and ditches under the roads, not to mention the broad, connecting Willamette, which carries all this water, even from streams high in the Cascades, downstream to the mighty Columbia and out to sea.

I savored the place names, the little towns I went through and the signs I saw pointing down other roads: Mulino, Canby, St. Paul, Champoeg, Newberg, Yamhill. Side roads led to Oregon City, Beaver Creek, and Silverton.

French Prairie is the historical name for the whole general area. The name of Molalla is associated with a local Indian tribe. The Willamette Valley itself is the heart of Oregon, where the native Kalapuyans once thrived and pioneer settlers formed the first provisional government in the Northwest.

In Canby, where a ferry still connects the east and west sides of the Willamette, I often stopped at an upscale coffee shop for coffee. There was a feeling of satisfaction at stomping in my muddy boots and rain jacket into this outpost of citified culture and ordering a hot latte or mocha for my drive home.

Crossing the Willamette River at Newberg, I felt a subtle difference between the east and west sides of the valley. On the east side of the valley the land climbs up and the vegetation changes. Because it is closer to the Cascades, it feels more like mountain country. To the west, the land seems dryer, with more oaks, and the mountains in view are the Coast Range, modest little mountains compared to the Cascades. There are plant nurseries on both sides—Oregon is a major producer of nursery plants—but I saw more vineyards at the west end of my drive. As the seasons changed, even in rain or icy weather, I loved watching the variations in color and light.

When I started the herding classes, I had some idea that I might train the dogs and use them to work our sheep at home, but as years went by we cut back on sheep. Even when we had up to thirty or forty sheep, and we let them out of the barn in the morning, they knew where they needed to take themselves to graze, depending on which adjoining gates were open or shut. During the years when we had more rams than made sense, six to be exact, the sheep generally sorted themselves. The ewes would graze and lie down together in one part of the field, and the rams would form their own little flock in a different area. At dusk, the sheep would make their way back to the barn on their own, mainly because they knew they would get a sweet snack of wet C.O.B., a feed consisting of corn, oats, and barley with a little molasses in the mix. Then the ewes marched confidently into the pen on the south side of the barn, and the rams went to the one on the north side. I don't know how they worked this out, but all we had to do was shut the gates behind them. Of course, this wasn't true at breeding time, when the ewes were coming into season, and the rams would develop oddly engorged, wrinkled noses and muzzles, a sign that they could smell which ewes were eligible. Then it was push and shove among the rams, who all wanted to get close to the ewes, each ram hoping to be selected as Prince Charming.

But we really didn't require herding dogs.

I only ever used the dogs to handle sheep if there was a breakout, and even then there wasn't much finesse to it, since the sheep, if they had gotten into the vegetable garden or a flower bed, would simply give an oh oh look at the sight of the dogs, turn around, and trot back where they belonged.

To tell the truth, I was reluctant to practice herding on my own sheep, even when they were more numerous and younger, because the whole practice is based on the predator and prey principle, and if the herding is awkward and the sheep aren't used to it, things can go wrong. Kathy's sheep were all very used to it. And perhaps in some ways I took the classes not only in order to learn from an expert about handling dogs but also in order to have someone else's sheep to pester. I sometimes wondered if the opportunities my dogs had to herd sheep brought out some obsessive characteristics that they wouldn't have shown otherwise. But border collies are instinctive herders. Herding has been bred into them for generations. Training brings discipline to the instinctive behavior.

Now that we no longer raise sheep, the only herding practice Maggie and Guy get is when the chickens are somewhere they shouldn't be. Also, when I go out to start the car without taking her, Maggie wants to run wide circles around it, as if trying to keep the car under control and in place. It's then that I think it would be nice to have a few dog-broke sheep.

The most important thing I learned in Kathy's classes, besides some useful commands, was a better understanding of how a herding dog thinks. I also learned something about the distinction between what a dog learns in order to get along with people, and what it knows deep down in its nature.

Who Goes There?

❖

It was late October. The dogs and I were poking around in the little woods below the vineyard. As we passed into the clearing where the wild apples grow, I saw a large and unfamiliar form of scat composed of half digested apples with a few berry seeds mixed in. It looked like apple pie filling, chewed but not formless, definitely not sauce. Further along the trail I saw a similar deposit.

Such are the wonders of the Internet that when I returned to the house and typed "scat" into my search engine I got several million hits, ranging from references to music to perverse recreations. So I narrowed the search to "identifying animal scat" and came up with a more relevant list. With the help of images and verbal descriptions, I confirmed that, as I suspected, the "apple pie" scat in our wild apple orchard had been left by a bear. We live just on the east side of the Oregon Coast Range and have occasionally seen small black bears in the area. Normally these bears are shy and stay away from populated areas, but even in our checker-boarded farm area there is plenty of woodland that provides a wild animal corridor into the Coast Range. Probably, a young bear learning to live on its own and looking for fruit at the end of summer caught the sweet smell of rotting apples and wandered onto our place for a while.

I had made another scat sighting not long before the one described above. One day the Barred Rock hen disappeared. The chickens generally stay close to their pen or at most venture into the pasture or into the yard to scratch apart my feeble efforts at creating a flower garden by the kitchen door. I checked the field for signs of feathers or carnage but didn't see anything.

A couple of days later, Bill and I were walking through the little oak woods. We wandered downhill, out of the oaks, through the new planting of small pines, and into the boggy ash swale at the bottom of the property. As we circled around and began the climb through the vineyard, I saw something in the middle of the trail that gave me a clue to the fate of our chicken.

Some animals, such as our sheep, nicely spread their random droppings as fertilizer over a large area. Others are modest, or at least selective in their private functions, going off into a thicket or a certain corner of a field. My husband tells me he once kept a pig that regularly selected one corner of its habitation as a toilet, and we know cats bury their scat. Even our dogs shyly prefer to go off into a grassy thicket or behind a bush, though they have twenty acres of open space. But not coyotes. Coyote scat is apt to be found right-splat on the public thoroughfare. If there's a path, they'll poop on it. Coyote apparently wants you to know that he or she has been there. Sometimes we see the coyotes themselves, but more often we see their sign on trails, the paths around nearby Hagg Lake, for example, as well as on our farm. Coyote scat is often threaded with the hair of rodents and bone fragments and returned to earth with a sort of spinner's twist. "Ha ha," says the coyote. "Missed me again."

On this particular afternoon, the color of the coyote scat looked peculiar so I bent to study it, wondering what the coyote had been eating. Embedded in the extrusion I saw a whole chicken toe, bright yellow and leathery, sharp toenail still attached—presumably the toe of our missing Barred Rock. I hoped that toenail gave the coyote a bellyache.

On another day I was driving along Russell Creek Road toward the highway when I saw a huge cat sauntering down the middle of the road in front of my car. I put on the brake and sat there. The cat must have weighed forty pounds or more and had a tail about eight inches long. I realized it was a big bobcat. It appeared to be as large as Guy and except for the tail I might have mistaken her for a young cougar. She paused in the road, turned momentarily to stare back at me over her shoulder, and then slipped like a shadow, off the road and into the fir trees on a neighbor's Christmas tree farm. A couple of days later I believe she paid me a visit closer to home, because in the driveway there was a deposit of scat much too large for a house-cat. It had been partially covered by a mound of gravel and dirt. But I didn't see the bobcat again.

We sometimes find owl pellets on the place. Once Eben, one of our grandchildren who was staying at the farm for the holidays, received a nicely packaged owl pellet from the Oregon Museum of Science and Industry for a Christmas present. The pellet came with a diagram of the different small animal bones that would likely be found in its composition. Owl pellets are not, strictly speaking, scat, because they are regurgitated rather than passed through the digestive system, but they are the detritus of the creature's recent meal. The science museum owl pellet came with a sorting dish and some small tools for dismantling and analysis. It was an interesting exercise and, perhaps even more interesting, the next day we were walking around outside when Eben suddenly spied a similar object under an oak tree in the top woods. We took it back to the house where, once dissected, it provided an assortment of tiny mouse and vole bones knit together with dry hair and other matter—similar to that in the commercially packaged pellet.

In addition to all of these digestive remnants, we sometimes know who has passed by from tracks in the muddy areas: signs of deer and quail, the small, hand-like prints of raccoons, the dragging tail and foot marks of pheasants, the prints of opossums. When we get one of our rare snowfalls, it is a revelation to go out before the dogs or the sheep have obliterated the evidence and see the tracks of skunks, deer, pheasants, and more.

One of our granddaughters was delighted when we found a snakeskin, about five feet long, in the grass below the vineyard. She arranged it as an exhibit in an old shoebox along with a photo of her holding the skin by the tail and a page of field notes—where the snake was found, date, length, etc.—and took it home to keep in her bedroom. I only wished we had been there to witness that gopher snake wriggling out of his long skin stocking. I would have liked to see how snakes do that trick.

Recently, we had a different sort of sighting. Up the center alley of the vineyard we found large hoof prints. Because of the hard rain and the fact that the area was more grassy than muddy, the prints weren't clear. We studied the tracks. When we were out walking the week before, a neighbor girl stopped her car to ask if we'd seen her runaway pony. It wasn't the first time someone had come by looking for a lost horse. I'm an optimist; maybe we had a pony in the woods. We walked farther down the hill and there the evidence was clear, as we came upon several large, soupy cow-plops. The neighbor's cow had jumped the fence again. Darn it. No pony.

Bear scat, snake skins, and owl pellets are more interesting than cow manure, but whatever creature crosses our land in the fog or rain or snow or dark of night, it's interesting to practice being amateur trackers. We often see deer, as well as their droppings, which resemble those of the sheep, and we both hear and see the owls that come out of the woods to hunt each night. We have seen our walnut tree full of raccoon babies, and California quail or pheasants often fly up out of the blackberry thickets. One day I saw a mink dodge down into the creek along nearby Stiller's Mill Road.

Occasionally a large primate leaves tracks in the neighborhood. Along our country road we sometimes find beverage bottles and fast food wrappers, or a mound of cigarette butts where someone has dumped a car ashtray. As much as possible, we toss the debris in with our garbage. One time someone scattered a truckload of old car tires along the verge of our road. It required the county road crew to clean that mess. Another time, just inside our fence line, we found a wad of nasty looking tissue. I imagined some county road worker finding himself too far from the nearest Sani-Can. There was nothing to do but haul out the shovel and bury it. Last winter a pair of men's blue undershorts showed up at the intersection of Lilac Hill and Goodrich Roads, near the southeast corner of our property.

Once in a while someone dumps the remains of an illegal deer or elk they have skinned and dressed out. A gory rib cage from such an animal decorated a thicket near the mushroom farm one winter until coyotes and turkey vultures tore it apart and cleaned it to white bone, which eventually disappeared into the dirt and blackberry vines. The traces we humans leave have a greater yuk factor than a pancake's worth of quickly dissolving, apple-laced bear scat, or the prints of claws and footpads on a muddy path.

I'm not sure what I would do if I came around a corner and saw a bear foraging among the wild apple trees. I will always look for one to show up again in October, when the bitter little apples fall into the tall grass or, on some trees, dangle bright red and lemon yellow, like glass Christmas ornaments, even after the leaves are long gone. It's illuminating to find evidence of the lines of locomotion all of us creatures make on the same ground, while only rarely coming face to face. I know they're out there, and I hope I get a chance to see that bobcat again, along with the rest of the locals that sometimes show up—quail, skunks, foxes, elk, even the splendid Tom turkey that once visited our pasture for a few days—but I never want to run into the guy who left his blue boxer shorts behind.

Coyote Wars

❖

Pinknose, the white Romney sheep, is staring hard at the bottom of the field. She has the look a sheep gives when she notices something unusual in the distance and is trying to figure out if it is cause for alarm. Bill moved the cross fences on Sunday, so perhaps she is wondering why she can no longer meander down to the apple trees along the property line, but our coyote problem has been bad this summer. Her stare makes me wonder if she sees a sinister movement in the thicket on the neighbor's place.

I am sick about the loss of lambs. When the first one was killed, we chalked it up to the occasional loss one might expect over years of raising sheep. We always put the sheep in the barn at night, the time when coyotes and loose dogs are most apt to be on the prowl. We keep the brush down along the fence lines to minimize stalking hideouts. In more than twenty years of raising sheep, we have had only the occasional problem with predation.

On the west side of our farm is an empty house; the owners have moved into town, and their field has grown up in Scotch broom, blackberry thickets, and grass. To the north of that, the woods belong to a widow, who frequently travels. Recently a neighbor down the road died. I think he was inclined to take out a shotgun when a coyote appeared. The silenced shotgun might explain the surge in coyote population. Mortality and absence, like ripples on a pond, spread their influence through the neighborhood.

Generally I don't like guns, and yet this summer the mixture of brush growth and no shooters had been a disaster for our sheep. Coyotes killed all five of this year's lambs plus Fudge, our frail, old ewe. One at a time they picked them off, not in the night, but

86

at midday, when we were at home and when the sheep were out munching the wild herbs and grasses in our sunny pasture or taking a lie-down to ruminate in the shade of the oak trees. All we had to do, it seemed, was turn our backs. Typically coyotes hunt small prey—rodents, rabbits, snakes. Both domestic and feral cats are coyote targets. Infrequently, a chicken has disappeared from our yard. Especially between July and September, when the female coyotes are teaching their pups to hunt, anything small can be prey. This is also the time when spring lambs are putting on size and weight and apt to wander away from their mothers or, if they are still nursing, taking naps in the tall grass while their browsing mothers drift farther and farther away in the field.

Most of our sheep are big enough to challenge a lone coyote or a single small dog. If they see something they perceive as danger—an unfamiliar person, a dog, or even a cat—the ewes move in front of their lambs and make stomping motions with their front feet. Of course, they are not fierce and will run if something actually comes after them, but a large sheep in full-fleece making hoof stomping gestures may not look like a likely victim to a coyote. This is not true, of course, for a lamb or a frail older sheep. After the first lamb was killed, we moved the sheep into the walnut grove near the house for a while, but then, hoping it was safe, we let them back into the big pasture where the grass was thicker and greener. That was a big mistake. After twenty years of raising sheep without problems, we had been lulled into a false security.

Even if you don't see the coyote her method is recognizable. The coyote is an expert killer, as one might expect from a species that has flourished near human society, in the absence of larger predators. She will go for the throat and take the lamb down, then dive into the belly and eviscerate the animal, pulling out the offal and laying it fastidiously aside as she dines on the choice organs: the heart, lungs, liver, and stomach. If she is undiscovered, she may come and go several times, eating until the lamb is reduced to bones, or she may tear off parts and drag them to a more private place. It is a horrible sign when turkey vultures appear in the trees at the bottom of the pasture. Smelling a coyote strike, they gather and wait their turn.

We don't shoot coyotes because we don't like to kill wild animals, coyotes have never been that big of a problem before, and we aren't gun lovers. But at times like this I think about it. Undoubtedly the number of kills on our lambs this summer will have trained this particular coyote and her pups to think of our farm as a free lunch counter. And yet I have sometimes watched with delight seeing a coyote hunting mice or voles in a nearby field—that intent hunting stare, the graceful high leap in tall grass, that pounce like a playful cat. Now I didn't know what to do, or rather, I wasn't sure what I wanted to do.

In late fall, about two months after four of our lambs had been killed, our last one was growing up nicely. We kept an eye on her and moved the sheep close to the house. But the last lamb had an unfortunate habit of wandering off and not sticking with the old sheep. She didn't rush to eat the alfalfa or grain in the barn, as the adult sheep did, but instead meandered away by herself in search of fresh grass. Numerous times I chased her back up the field to join the rest of the flock.

One day I watched Bill come up the yard with the wheelbarrow and go to the plowed area at the back of the garden. I went out and asked him what was going on.

"I didn't want to tell you I was burying our last lamb," he said. My heart clenched. She was my sweet lamb that marched around with a sheep smile on her placid face; my lamb I had imagined raising to replenish our dwindling and geriatric flock. For a moment I knew what it was to scream at the heavens. It felt like the story of Beowulf. Grendel had struck again. I woke that night with a sad and heavy feeling. The last of the year's lambs was gone.

Admittedly, we raised some of the lambs for meat as well as wool, or we sold them to others who might keep them for wool and as pets, but who also might raise them for food. If you are a meat eater and have the space and facilities, raising your own lamb may be the ideal way to assure that what you eat is wholesome and was treated humanely in its short life of eight-to-twelve months. Either way, wool or meat, this was our lamb, not the coyote's. Again, I thought of a shotgun, but in the back of my mind was also the thought that since there were no more lambs, we probably didn't have to worry about coyote predation any more this year. Next year we would do better somehow.

There is always a feeling of guilt when something bad happens to livestock. The animals are under our protection. One asks, what could I have done? What did I do wrong? Bill did a major clean up of brush along the fence, and we let the adult sheep back into the main pasture. Fall was coming on.

One day I looked toward the west field and saw the turkey vultures gathering in the tree on the neighbor's brushy property. In the woods I heard crows cawing. I called the dogs and ran down the field. A coyote bolted along the fence and jumped over, disappearing into the thick undergrowth of the neighbor's field. It was horrible to find the carcass of Fudge, at sixteen our oldest sheep. The sheep's head and legs, still covered with her soft gray wool, were pulled aside. The coyote—or coyotes, because I could hardly believe one coyote alone had made such short work of her—had raked the carcass to the ribs and spine. It is unusual to lose an adult sheep to coyotes, but Fudge was so old and frail, she had been easy prey.

Fudge was the daughter of Toffee, one of our original sheep, and looked just like her. Along with the other sheep, she had been sheared not long ago. Even though Fudge's wool had grown too coarse and sparse to make good wool for spinning, we felt shearing was for her own good. We got the Romneys originally because of their luxuriant wool. Unlike the coats of hair sheep, the fleece on a wool sheep grows and grows. It does a good job of protecting the animals from winter rains and cold, but it can also be a problem, especially with the older sheep, when it is too heavy. When older sheep get more than a year's growth and it rains, their wool get water-soaked and they sometimes have a hard time standing up. Or, weighted by too much wool, they roll over on their backs on the hillside and can't get back on their feet. And yet I cursed the shearing when I considered that had Fudge still had her long fleece it might have kept the coyote from getting a hold on her.

We buried Fudge, and my mind went in circles about what to do. Was I through with raising sheep? Much as I loved it, it was hard work and a lot of emotional investment. I wasn't getting any younger, and maybe it was time to plant trees in the pasture instead. For two days I kept the sheep in the barn and fed them on alfalfa, but eventually I had to let them into the field. Bill gave me dark looks when I ranted about the coyote problem. He too felt helpless and frustrated with the coyote attacks. He had worked hard on new fencing and clearing brush, and it had done no good.

One morning he said he had a plan for changing the cross fencing. It would keep the sheep out of the lower part of the pasture and away from the property line where brush provided a dense cover for hunting coyotes. He spent a long day pulling and repositioning posts and moving wire fencing. The pasture is now smaller, but we can see the sheep more easily as they browse and no longer lose sight of them like we used to when they were able to move over the brow of the hill. We don't know if it will stop the problem. I am still thinking about shotguns or calling a trapper, but I don't like those solutions either.

Like any creature, a coyote has its own life and nature. Coyotes are native to North America, unlike domestic sheep that have been bred from old world varieties. Native North American sheep in general have not been domesticated, and they are not farm animals. The ancestors of domestic sheep, such as island breeds of sheep in the UK, or sheep from desert areas in the Middle East, generally enjoy habitats without large predators. And even here, coyotes largely make their meals off small prey, such as mice, voles, or rabbits. In a sense, coyote predation of sheep is a result of human practice.

Coyote plays a major role in American Indian tradition. Coyote is a lively anti-hero and mythic figure in Native American folklore, a trickster who both hinders and helps human beings. He is not unlike Loki and Prometheus in European mythologies. Sometimes Coyote fools people or other animals, sometimes he is fooled. In one Nez Perce story, Coyote is given the chance to bring his beloved wife back from the land of the dead, but like Orpheus who tried and failed to lead his wife out of the underworld, Coyote is unable to restrain his impulses, and he loses her forever. Thereafter, the myth tells us, the dead are irrecoverable, not only for Coyote but for humanity as well. I think of my irrecoverable sheep.

I would like to be able to live with coyotes without it becoming a range war and for over twenty years we were able to do so. It is hard to think of giving up the beautiful sight of a line of sweet sheep moving out of the barn in the morning and into the long grass, but to tell the truth, I am thinking about getting out of the sheep game altogether.

A Tale of Two Roosters

❖

The Barred Rock rooster had done the unforgivable. He flew across the chicken coop and buried a spur in the back of my leg. I threw the water bucket at him, missed, and stumbled into the house to take care of my wound.

We didn't intend to raise any roosters. When we got the chicks a year ago in the spring, we ordered hens, but as they grew, Bill speculated that we might have a couple of roosters.

I knew he was probably right, but I didn't want it to be true and said it was impossible.

But it was possible. The roosters were soon noticeably larger than the hens and developed grand red combs. One of them was a Black Australorpe, his ebony plumage tinged with green and purple iridescence, his tail a fall of glistening feathers in constant quivering motion. The other was a Barred Rock with gleaming red, gold, and blue threads streaking his mantle above the dominant pattern of black and white.

Roosters aren't good for much if you don't care about fertile eggs and don't want your hens to hatch new chicks, but they have their own lives and can be as beautiful as any bird in the world. I often admired the roosters as they paraded around the yard, leading the charge to scratch for birdseed under the wild bird feeders and crowing now and then, apropos of nothing we could recognize. The hens put up with the roosters' wild morning amours and then did their best to stay out of their way. Roosters are often naturally feisty and in some cultures cockfighting is a popular spectator sport. The last state to outlaw cockfighting in the United States was Louisiana in 2007. But the last thing we wanted was a cockfight on our hands. The young roosters got in a couple of squabbles without doing any visible damage. After that Blacky became the boss rooster, and Rocky backed down when they seemed headed for any kind of conflict.

Blacky was my favorite rooster. The wave-like torrent of his shining black tail feathers with their green-and-purple highlights quivered in the sunlight, and his enormous red comb contrasted dramatically with his blue-black plumage. Besides being beautiful, he was rather courteous with the females. When he wanted to court a hen he circled her in a complicated and graceful dance, doing odd little rooster curtsies and dragging one wing dramatically in the dust. I could almost hear the flamenco music as I watched him.

We often let the chickens out of the pen so that they had free range of the flower beds and lawn, eating grass and bugs and scratch-ing in the gravel of the driveway. Sometimes they got way too en-thusiastic and ended up digging a plant out of the garden, but for the most part they did little damage. I figured they were doing more good than harm by eating slugs and other pests.

Late in the spring, coyotes again started showing up on the place, and our old hen, Onesie, disappeared. She was from the last batch of chickens and had outlived the others by at least a couple of years. Onesie was from a bunch of Ameraucana hens we had raised from chicks when my grandson Eben was a toddler, and he had named them, appropriately, Onesie, Twosie, Threesie, and so on. I think we had six in that group, as I don't remember a Sevensie or Eightsie. I hated to think that old Onesie had succumbed to a fox or coy-ote, and I worried about the younger chickens. We decided to keep them penned, but they soon realized they could fly over the fence. Of course, they couldn't seem to figure out how to fly back in at night so we ended up with roosting chickens in the trees and in the barn. After another chicken disappeared we bought some netting to put over the chicken yard. But before we could spread the netting, what was probably a coyote struck again, and we found Rocky's feathers strewn across the sheep pasture.

I followed the trail of black and white feathers, thinking that I might at least find his body though I had no hope of finding him alive. The feathers led to the fence line where I could see the hint of a trail under the barbed wire. The trail led through an acre of brush and beyond that through a minefield of poison oak and then into the oak woods on our neighbor's property. There I gave up.

I walked slowly back to the house. As I topped the hill I heard a faint, familiar rawk rawk. It was the sound of a discontented chicken. Turning, I saw Rocky in the distance, approaching the barnyard with measured dignity. He came all the way to the hen house, step by martial step, rawk rawking all the way. When he turned and entered the hen yard I saw that his tail feathers were gone, and on his bald butt was the mark of a coyote's bite. I wondered what had happened to the coyote in that fight.

Though I rejoiced at Rocky's victorious return, we had one more disaster. Though we had draped the chicken yard with netting, Blacky got out somehow. There was a telltale pile of black feathers right at the barn door. The coyote must have come upon him by approaching from the back of the barn rather than across the pasture, snatched him, and taken off. There was no miraculous return for Blacky.

After we managed to confine the chickens for the most part to the poultry yard and hen house, we had no more trouble with the coyote, but Rocky began to strut his stuff as he stepped into the dominant place left by Blacky, who had always behaved in a most gentlemanly manner. Rocky became more and more aggressive, diving at the back of my jeans if I wasn't cautious when I went to gather eggs. I wondered if his victorious escape from the coyote had gone to his beautiful but brainless little head. His aggressions reminded me of our geese, long gone but well remembered, and how the sign of a retreating back was always a sign for them to attack. A gander's bite can hurt, but it can't hold a candle to the pain inflicted by a rooster's spurs, which are like boning knives.

I learned this lesson all too well that day when I went into the chicken house without adequate caution, and before I knew it I was howling with pain as Rocky buried a spur in the back of my right calf. I whirled around and threw the water bucket in his direction, which sent him running across the yard but didn't make me feel any better.

Back in the house I washed my wound with an iodine scrub, put antibiotic ointment on it, and then covered it with a bandage. But it didn't bleed that much, and there really was no good way to clean out the hole in my leg. I should have known that wasn't enough to treat a puncture wound.

I was not happy with Rocky. Bill offered to chop the rooster's head off if I would pluck him, but I didn't want to make any rash decisions. Hoping to pass on the burden of a decision I said, "You do what you want with him." Whereupon he said, "It's not my rooster."

Lucky me.

I was busy the next day and hoped the wound would heal, but my leg grew stiffer and sorer. By Saturday night it was hot, red, and swollen, and I could hardly walk. Sunday morning I called the hospital emergency line, and the on-call doctor said he would phone in a prescription for an antibiotic, which I could pick up at the nearest pharmacy. I took my medicine and hobbled around the rest of the day feeling sorry for myself and mad at the rooster.

He, of course, didn't know I was mad at him. He continued to run gleefully to the gate as if I were Santa Claus when I tossed in cantaloupe seeds and rinds left from our lunch. When we were face to face he would fix his golden eye on me in a bland, totally neutral way. He is a creature of instinct I told myself. This behavior is his nature. Should he be killed for acting on his nature?

The trouble is, almost no one wants a rooster, so there was no question of passing on this problem to anyone else. I would guess even the Humane Society doesn't want a rooster. Chickens for most people are food. Fried chicken. Roast chicken. Chicken salad. Chicken nuggets. Chicken burritos and the mysterious fast food "chicken fingers." We don't kill our own chickens since they provide us with entertainment and fresh eggs, but we do eat chicken raised elsewhere. At a year and a half, Rocky was probably too old for a tender fryer—fryers are short-lived eating machines that have been bred to mature in a matter of weeks—but perhaps Rocky was meant for soup. The trouble was, my mind kept saying get rid of that rooster while my emotions were saying, he is so beautiful, and especially, he did fight off a coyote.

On Monday when I returned to work at the college, my leg felt terrible, and I could hardly make it up and down the stairs to my office. When people saw me limping and asked me what had happened, instead of being able to say something exciting such as that I'd had a skiing accident or fallen off my skateboard or even, a respectable if rather pathetic possibility, that I'd fallen on the stairs and twisted my ankle, I had to blurt out: my rooster attacked me.

Now what was so funny about a rooster attack? My students were all in giggles. They wanted to see my wound with their own eyes, perhaps to see if it justified my limping and complaints, but, a little huffily, I told them to forget it. I wasn't going to become a spectacle. We had planned a creative writing walking field trip that day, but I wasn't in any shape to walk so I gave them their writing assignment and sent them out on their own. They viewed this dismissal as a cause for jollity and left with the assignment in hand, saying, take care of your rooster bite. Bite indeed.

Some people looked at me with sympathetic eyes but weren't sure whether they ought to say anything: I could almost imagine them thinking, my, she's looking decrepit. Other people snickered when I explained the mishap. I responded as politely as I could and even laughed myself. But the question still bothered me. What to do with that rooster? I thought of his heroic escape from the coyote. And the way the sunlight sparkled so beautifully on the red and blue, thread-like feathers in his mantle, and on the neat black-and-white checkerboard of his Barred Rock pattern. What was most important? Caution? Beauty? Revenge? Survival of the fittest? Common sense? What was one rooster more or less?

I looked online to see if there was any information about getting roosters to behave besides chopping their heads off, but no one suggested the rooster equivalent of neutering a feisty male dog. I realized that I had not really understood the damage a rooster could do, or how he would do it, before getting the point of his spurs myself. Earlier the same rooster had flown at my grandson and scratched his stomach. It hurt, obviously, but Eben braved through it. I treated the small, red mark with iodine and antibiotic, but I was naïve enough about roosters to think it was the mark of the rooster pecking with his beak. Now I realized that, like the fighting cocks one hears about in traditions or infrequently in news stories, and sees memorialized in Italian wine iconography, the rooster attacks with his spurs.

The spur is a kind of toe-like appendage that builds up layers of cartilage as the rooster gets older and the spur gets stronger. When I looked at one farm woman's online blog, I found a strange antidote for spurs. Here is what she prescribed as a remedy for a dangerous rooster: First you bake a potato. While the potato is still steaming hot, you catch the rooster. You then push the rooster's spurs, one at a time, into the hot potato and leave them there for a few minutes, being careful, she cautions, not to burn the rooster on the leg. I had a hard time imagining Rocky putting up with this treatment, but I read on. After ten minutes or so of the spur baking in the hot potato, she said, remove the potato, and you will find that the tough outer covering of the rooster's spur will easily slide off leaving only a tender little appendage, no longer dangerous.

I did not try this remedy.

So what did I do with the rooster? While thinking of how to end this tale, I recalled another old story, involving two doors. Behind one was a lady. Behind the other was a tiger. So in the end, which would it be? Which would you choose for the rooster? The guillotine, the hot potato? Hope he would grow out of it, simply avoid him? The lady or the rooster?

The Old Sheep

Last night Nancy, the old sheep, died. I'm not sure how old she was, and in fact I'm not even sure she was Nancy because according to our naming system that would have made her twelve years old, and I'm fairly sure she was at least two years older than that. I think we might have actually sold Nancy years ago. If this sounds careless, I admit that in the later years of sheep-rearing I became less scrupulous about the alphabetical system we used to keep track of individual ewes and offspring than I was twenty-five years ago and just starting out.

When it really matters, sheep breeders sometimes use numbered ear tags, clipped to a pierced ear, to sort out their sheep identities. Because many of our sheep were varicolored with distinctive markings it was easy to tell them apart. Early on even the all-white sheep seemed to have distinctive faces—some with larger eyes and fluttering eyelashes, others with more narrow noses, one with a black spot on her nose, one with especially alert, forward-set ears, one with a distinctive ruff and clean forehead, and so on. I still remember many of their faces: Cleo, our delicate, bottle-fed triplet, the prettiest of all; Aurora with her aristocratic Roman nose; Beauregard with his immense head, golden eyes, and deep brownfleece . . . We didn't follow the practice of clipping tags to their ears but just depended on recognizing them. I don't know if I became jaded over the years, but I do know that eventually there was a small group of closely related sheep that were more uniform. I had a hard time telling apart three white ewes. So now I simply called the remaining ewe from that group of three Nancy, whether she was Nancy or not. Whoever she was, I do know she was a survivor sheep, having weathered several mishaps including a severe infection after one year's lambing. In a later incident she became entangled in a woven-wire fence. She somehow stuck her leg through the fence and then fell over, thrashing around and scraping her leg raw before we found her. We carefully lifted her into a wheelbarrow for a ride up to the barn, put her in a small pen, and administered antibiotic ointment and penicillin shots. But the infection raged, and she seemed so close to death that Bill—a practical man, knowing he would be busy the next day—dug a grave in the hard summer ground before nightfall.

That night I got up several times to salve her wounds and, hoping to give her the energy to hold on, gave her doses of glycol with an old turkey baster. Nancy could barely lift her head. She developed a drawn, dehydrated appearance, and began to breathe with a ragged sound. I dribbled water down her throat with the ever-handy turkey baster, pushed clean straw around her head as a kind of pillow, filled an empty gallon milk carton with hot water to serve as a hot water bottle against her back, and covered her with a warmed blanket. The next morning when we went out to the barn she was sitting upright, and when I took her a basin of molasses-flavored C.O.B., she nibbled it enthusiastically with a happy crunch, crunch, crunch sound. By afternoon she was amazingly on her feet again. Bill grimly left the grave open for a while just in case, but we didn't need it.

Once I asked a vet how long sheep normally live. She said she didn't know because most people don't keep old sheep. So I don't know how usual it is for sheep to live to between thirteen and fifteen years, as our pet sheep usually did. When I looked up sheep longevity on the Internet the estimate was nine to twelve years, but there were no distinctions between ewes and rams, pets, or sheep sent to auction. Some breeds, such as Merinos, live longer than others, and I found reports of sheep living past twenty. Our sheep met their ends in various ways: peacefully in their sleep; sometimes traumatically in a dog or coyote attack; a couple of times in a sudden collapse after lambing. A few times we had to call in a vet to administer a final, humane injection to a failing and arthritic old sheep. We have raised many lambs, but over the years our flock usually consisted of between ten or fifteen ewes, beginning with Amity, Aurora, Why, and Toffee, their offspring, which we kept, and two or three rams. At the most, in a big lambing year, we had thirty or more sheep on the place and then sold the lambs. Much as I loved raising sheep, it was sometimes hard work and always sad when something went wrong. We began to pull back from the sheep business, especially after the two years of incessant coyote attacks. One by one our elderly sheep died. So now we were down to two retired ewes on the place.

Though I am not sure how old Nancy was when she died, I know her teeth were worn down almost to the gums, one reason for the decline of old sheep. Grazing, especially in the dry summer when grass may be dusty or gritty, is hard on sheep's teeth. When their teeth wear down naturally they have difficulty getting enough nutrition from grazing. We supplemented the two old ewes' diet with grain sweetened with molasses, but chewing was still a slow process.

Nancy also seemed to be arthritic and had difficulty bending down to graze. With arthritis in my own thumbs and feet, I could sympathize with that. We kept Nancy's feet trimmed, like all our sheep, and she never had foot rot, nor did any of our other sheep ever have that nasty ailment, but instead of standing she often went down on her knees to feed. I speculated that the episode of getting tangled in the fence might have left her with a sore leg. In any case, she had a stiff, elderly walk. She did seem happy to wander in and out of the barn, however, and to go out in the pasture to graze every day with her companion Pink Nose.

After many years, Pink Nose was our other remaining sheep, another old ewe. Her name did not conform to our usual alphabetical pattern of naming but simply described the fact that, unlike most Romneys, which have black noses, her nose was pink. Pink Nose and Nancy were old friends and went everywhere together, grazing or lying down to ruminate. Sheep are flock animals that enjoy the companionship of other sheep. After years of observing sheep behavior and the way they paired up for lying down or grazing, I realized that sheep do have friends.

When I thought about buying some new starter sheep, I had to remind myself that we had been through over twenty years of lambing, shearing, hoof trimming, medicating, fence mending, and general haul-ass work; we weren't getting any younger. As far as raising lambs to sell or eat, I found that I had come to dread the inevitable arrival of the butcher. Animal scientist Temple Grandin, who works with slaughter animals, makes the point that most farm animals would not exist if they were not needed for meat. I still believed that humane animal rearing and slaughter were possible, and necessary so long as people continue to eat meat, but we were eating more and more vegetables from our garden and often, though not always, ate vegetarian meals.

For years we had named the sheep that were to become our stock and in essence our pets, but we didn't name the ones we planned to sell or eat. Sometimes a forty-dollar leg of lamb in the market called to mind the luxury that was once abundant in our freezer. But it was a lot of work, and I had mixed feelings. The two old pet sheep somehow served as place markers while we decided whether or not to restock and start over. In the meantime, we had become a sheep retirement facility. One starry night when Bill went out to close the two sheep into the barn, they hadn't come up from the field. He walked downhill. As I started off to check the other end of the field he called, "Here she is."

"Is she okay?" I called back.

"*Morte*," was his succinct answer.

I walked across the recently mown pasture. It had been a wet spring, and even though it was the end of July there was still a lot of fresh grass coming, enough to feed a flock of sheep. But there was no longer a flock of sheep to feed.

Nancy lay in the grass where she had died, looking like she was just sleeping. Pink Nose was standing nervously at hand, unwilling to leave her longtime companion until Bill shooed her into the barn. Now Pink Nose was alone for the first time in her life, the last sheep of our flock. I worried about her being alone. For a moment I thought about going to the auction to buy another sheep to keep her company, or perhaps I should find someone else to take her into their flock. I wondered how I would feel, no longer raising sheep after so many years. It was a strange feeling. Momentarily I felt depressed at how quickly life goes by.

A mixture of such thoughts passed through my mind as Bill went to the barn to find a shovel. It had been five years since he dug Nancy's first, unused grave. Once again the summer heat had dried the clay beneath our pasture to a brick-like consistency.

"Farewell Nancy," I said, when we had laid her to rest with a clutch of flowers on her grave. There were many other sheep bones in this field. Sheep hate to be alone, and she wouldn't be. Bill's comment was, "Why do they always have to do this when the ground is so damn hard."

The Downfall of Boss Rooster

❖

Last spring I got another small batch of chicks to augment my dwindling flock, which consisted of one old rooster and three elderly hens. This old rooster was Rocky, the same guy who had stabbed me with his spurs in his youth, but now that he was about seven or eight years old he had mellowed considerably. Of course, I never wanted a rooster in the first place, but according to the clerk at the feed store, the people who sex chicks are only about 90 percent accurate. I hoped for better luck with the new batch, but unfortunately chicks are very tiny and a little ambiguous on the backside.

One day when the chicks were a few weeks old, Bill said, "I know you don't want to hear this . . ." I hate it when Bill starts sentences with "I know you don't want to hear this," because I surely don't, but I looked at him and waited for whatever doomsday statement he was about to make. "I know you don't want to hear this," he repeated, "but I think one of those chicks is a rooster."

I protested that it couldn't be. One in six isn't 10 percent, and besides, I didn't want another rooster. Alas, wishful thinking does not turn a rooster into a hen. So eventually we had another rooster marching around the place and giving the hens trouble. The young and old roosters did not seem hostile to one another—no cockfights going on—so I ignored suggestions from unfeeling friends about making rooster soup and let them be.

Then one dark day Bill came in with his bearer-of-bad-news look and told me he thought the old rooster was dead. I went out to the pen. It had been raining—soppy, late-winter, Oregon rain— and the old rooster lay on the ground covered with mud. I'd let the chickens out during the day so they weren't confined to the pen, but if any grass sprouted in the chicken yard at this point in the year they ate it. The ground inside the fence had been scratched and pecked and rained on until it was a bog. The rooster looked as if someone had used him to mop up the muck and then plastered him to the ground with it. I bent down to study him more closely. He definitely looked dead. Then suddenly, like a scene in a horror movie, the mud opened one eye and looked unblinking right at me.

From his pecked and bloody head I knew the young rooster had attacked him. Then I saw another mud-covered and only slightly less bloody rooster come marching around the corner of the chicken house. This one was strutting and crowing in spite of the mud. I chased him away and went back to the house for a towel, with which I wrapped up the old rooster and carried him off out of cock-range.

I gave Rocky a brisk rubdown and set him on the grass in the fenced backyard. He stood there unsteadily for a few moments, finally settling into a crouching position under the viburnum bush. I put an antibiotic salve on his raw head, set out water and food nearby, and waited to see what would happen.

For a few days he seemed content to stay in his safe haven, and the peck marks on his head began to heal. The weather had cleared, and he was able to shake off much of the mud that coated his feathers. Perhaps he could live out his remaining days in the backyard. I worried a little that the dogs would bother him, but though they usually enjoy giving a chicken a scare, they found the rooster too uninteresting to bother after they sniffed him over a time or two.

One day he disappeared, and we couldn't find any sign of him. No loose feathers or gore to indicate a predator, and no corpse to explain why he didn't come to his dish.

I am always interested to know how long any critters on the place are apt to survive, and nowadays it's easy to get some idea from searching the Internet. I typed in "chicken life expectancy." Some sources said five to seven years; others said a chicken can live into its teens, under good conditions. Our chickens are well fed and housed in a coop at night. They get a lot of freedom in the day to roam the pasture and find happy chicken snacks—fresh grass, bugs, worms, and so on. Our experience has been that chickens do not have lingering illnesses. Once in a while a chicken falls off the stoop; I use the phrase both literally and metaphorically. We hear a squawk, then a thump, and by the time we go in to see what's happened the chicken is already stiff and cooling on the floor. I assume this is some version of a chicken heart attack or stroke. Maybe it's a good way to go.

The other way we have lost chickens is an occasional predator attack. A chicken simply disappears during the day. It's a calculated risk to let them roam free. I have seen a fox come up the driveway and head for the chicken house in broad daylight, and there was the time the Barred Rock hen disappeared, and at the bottom of the vineyard I found the coyote scat colorfully accented with a leathery yellow toe. But because we shut the chickens in the henhouse at night, they are usually safe from predators.

Because this old rooster was close to eight years old, I thought he might have reached the end of his life span, especially considering the trauma of the attack and his sudden dethroning as chief cock of the walk. But I knew he had to be somewhere, so I continued to look for him in the fenced backyard, with no luck. Then, a couple of days after the rooster had disappeared, Bill was putting the other chickens in for the night when he saw a needle-like beak sticking out from a tiny crack behind the egg boxes. Somehow the old rooster had managed to get out of the backyard, into the chicken house, and then had mysteriously inserted himself through a minute space between the egg boxes and the wall in order to hide from the bullying young rooster. I couldn't even imagine how he got in there. It took the two of us to move the heavy, double-decker chicken boxes to get him out. I returned him to the backyard. There he had fresh grass, a nice place under the deck to get in out of the weather, the security of a fence, and all the food and water he could use. He should have been content to stay, but I could see he had lost his spirit.

He lived in the backyard for a while, occasionally flying over the fence and appearing out front, but after his one return to the chicken house he never went back. Somehow he reminded me of Wallace Beery, a worn-out boxer in the old movie The Kid, and other times I thought of him as the fallen Lear or a deposed general. His feathers were never as nice after that mud bath, and even after he shed the dirt they still looked lackluster. Though the wounds on his head healed, his comb had lost its fulsome splendor and was ragged and limp. His claws and spurs, which in his youth had done such damage to the back of my leg, looked blunted and rough, leathery and dull. He was a sad looking rooster, but I hoped he found some comfort at the watering bucket, where he stood for long periods sipping and gargling. He reminded me of my long-ago pecked and exiled chicken Scalpina, who had lived out her days with the geese after a similar beating in the chicken yard, that time by her sister hens. As much as I like my chickens, I admit they are capable of very bad behavior. Henpecked is not just an expression.

Rocky did end up living out the rest of his days in the backyard, but he was never a happy bird. I think he lost the will to live once his kingdom and harem were taken away from him. On reflection, I wonder if I should have moved one of the old hens into the yard to keep him company—the one with the saggy bosom and the cultured but quavering voice, who sometimes reminded me of an elderly army wife in a flowered dress and pearls.

The Proof Is in the Blackberry Pudding

❖

The air is hot and still. All around Yamhill County, hay lies baled and ready to be stored in barns. Something sweet and fruity mixes with the dry grass smell in the air and tells me to go looking for the old blackberry pudding recipe.

My recipe drawer is chaotic—I can't find the recipe. I have a dim memory of having placed the berry-stained, three-by-five card between pages of one of my recipe books, maybe the falling-to-pieces copy of *The Joy of Cooking* that I got when I moved into my first apartment in college in 1960, or maybe *The Good Housekeeping Cook Book,* a long-ago wedding present from a different marriage.

Each of my cookbooks has specific memories and distinctive stain marks. In *The Joy of Cooking,* the most grease spots are on the page for "Fruit Paradise," a superior kind of apple cobbler. In *The Good Housekeeping Cook Book,* which has long lost its cover and the index following "u," the tamale pie page is similarly greasy. In my more recent *The New York Times Cookbook,* another possible hiding place for the blackberry pudding recipe, the scone page is heavily marked with flour and butter. I see a trend here. Even more of my favorite recipes exist on scraps of paper, file cards, or yellowed clippings taken from newspapers. Organizing recipes is not my style, though sometimes I wish it were.

What if I've lost it? Panicked, I dial Mom's number. I know she'll have it, but she doesn't answer. My husband discovers me tossing recipe papers this way and that. He sometimes calls himself "Bill the Finder," when I call on him to help me locate glasses, car keys, and other lost objects. I am happy to let him keep his title, so long as he is willing to search. In a few minutes he finds the recipe on a wrinkled piece of old-style computer paper with holes along the edge. I was sure it was on a card. I must have copied it more than once.

I should have the directions memorized by now, but there's something about the nuances of the wording that requires reading the recipe itself. Here it is:

Blackberry Pudding
sift 1 c flour, ½ c sugar, 1 large t baking powder, salt (pinch)

cut in 1 large T fat

add ½ c milk

spread thin dough on greased baking dish

add 2 <u>or more</u> c berries

cover with 1 c sugar

pour on top 1 c+ boiling water

bake 375 degrees 45 min or less

I like the imprecision of the recipe. The teaspoon of baking powder is "large." I interpret that as heaping. The tablespoon of shortening is also "large," and it is described simply as "fat," which reminds me that when my mom got the recipe from our friend, Helen Starr, we lived in Clatskanie, Oregon, during World War II. With wartime rationing it was the patriotic custom to save cooking fat, whether it was lard, butter, or meat dripping. "Fat" was "fat," and a large tablespoon of bacon drippings or used fry grease could be used as well as some other processed, hard to find "fat." The salt is a "pinch," which I have always understood as the amount you can pinch between thumb and forefinger without losing it. The berries in the recipe are described as "2 or more" cups. The precise amount is up to the cook. I've often used as many as four cups of blackberries. The boiling water, which is poured over the concoction before it goes into the oven, is described as "1 c+," so there is a certain leeway there as well, though if the berries are extra juicy too much water can make the dish soupy.

An interesting feature of the recipe is that the prepared dough goes in first, on the bottom, but as the dish cooks the dough rises to the top of the berries and creates islands of delicious browned pastry in the thickened fruit.

It seems an infallible recipe to me, but at least one family friend said she was never able to make it come out the way my mother did. I can't account for that. She may have needed more precise directions.

Perhaps, for me, some of the pleasure of the dessert lies in the associations it evokes. I can't make this pudding without remembering Helen Starr, who was a wonderful old-fashioned cook. She and her husband, Paul, or Doctor Starr, were family friends in Clatskanie. Our family moved there during World War II, when I was four years old. Both my family and the Starrs belonged to a small sailing club in those gas-rationing days. At the end of summer, the road to the boathouse slough was thick with the sweet odor of blackberries. Of course, thinking of Helen also reminds me of the taste of her buckwheat pancakes, her dumplings with stewed wild duck (Doc Starr was a duck hunter), and the sour cream fudge, which she cooled on a white marble slab in her pantry. But for me, blackberry pudding was always at the apex of her culinary delights.

Associations of place with the recipe are many. I think of the boathouse, where the banks of the slough were covered with blackberry brambles, and the boat ride out into the Columbia to the far side of Wallace Island. Clatskanie was a remote place back then. I remember the slow and winding old roads that connected the town to larger places—Portland, Longview, Astoria. They were all too far to go for routine medical care, and so, in 1945, my little brother was delivered by Helen's husband in the tiny hospital ward above a bank.

Across the street from our house in Clatskanie was a field of grass and blackberry thickets where my friends and I carved hideouts in the thorny vines, somehow without getting scratched to death. In the shade of a domed thicket we would sit picking hot blackberries from overhead and imagining that we could survive there by living on wild fruit, at least for the summer.

Questions of survival had a sharp poignancy in those days, since World War II was a constant presence even in that idyllic and remote western place. My father was the only telephone repairman for miles around; besides providing general service, he took care of the wartime ammunition dump outside Clatskanie. After being drafted, he was sent back home to us since there was no other telephone man available to keep the lines up and running. I would sometimes ride along with him in the telephone truck when he went into the country to set poles or find trouble on a line. There, too, the roads were lined with dust-covered blackberry bushes. I remember quail dashing out of the thickets and across the road into the safety of more brambles. The perfume of berries was overwhelming.

I know that blackberry vines can be a curse if you're trying to clear land or keep them out of your yard. Some people keep goats, or use herbicide and bulldoze fields, just to get rid of them. We have been chopping them off our fences forever. Their vigor seems unmatched and though there is a trailing, smaller, native variety, most of the wild blackberries around are non-natives, Himalayan or Evergreen. Both were brought from Western Europe, perhaps as late as the mid-nineteenth century, but it seems they have been here a long time, and the gift of the fruit is sweet. A friend, who lived along the Umpqua River, credited the untended thickets of Himalayan blackberries—some with canes over twenty feet long—for saving his cabin from washing away, as many other places actually did in the great flood of 1964. Neighboring houses went sailing away, but not Ferguson's cabin behind the blackberry wall. Maybe he was right. One of my favorite parts of the recipe is that underlining of "or more." The underlining is in my mother's handwritten version of the recipe, and I have always interpreted this to mean that more is better where blackberries are concerned. The final direction, "bake 375 degrees 45 min or less," also suggests old-fashioned, seat-of-the-pants cooks, who know the true temperature of an oven and when a dessert is done, however long it takes. In wartime, when my mother first got the recipe from Helen, we still had a wood cook stove.

We usually eat the blackberry pudding after dinner, hot or cold, with ice cream or whipped cream or with nothing at all. In the unlikely event that there's a tiny bit left in the corner of the rectangular Pyrex baking dish, whoever is up first in the morning eats it for breakfast.

Every August the family convenes on the southern Oregon coast, which became home a few years after we left Clatskanie. No one in the family actually lives there anymore, but we still have a wooded hideaway for summer camping. At the end of our camping sojourn, my grown children and the young grandchildren collect blackberries with coffee tins or beach buckets, pack them in ice chests, and hurry them though the August heat back to their various city homes to be frozen for blackberry pudding when days gets cooler and summer's abundance is a memory.

At this point I should say that in my family we use the word cobbler and pudding interchangeably in referring to this dish. In Oregon, various styles of blackberry cobbler, or pudding, or crisp, frequently show up at end-of-summer potlucks, but to me no other version tastes as good as this one. Biscuit topping is heavy and lacks the slight crunch and texture of the old blackberry pudding recipe. Overly sweet crisp obscures the fruit. Really, there is no comparison. The fact that there's nothing exactly like Helen's blackberry pudding recipe in any of my cookbooks makes me wonder. Searching the Internet I found two similar versions, though neither was quite the same.

So here's to Helen Starr: thanks for the memories and the recipe. Let us go out into the sweet-smelling sun, with a bucket and a big straw hat, and gather ripe berries as if there were no other day and no other meaning to life than the fruit on the vine and the pudding in the pan.

Equinox Soup

❖

Late September, the autumnal equinox. I open the refrigerator door and wonder what to cook for dinner. The refrigerator looks messy, too many odds and ends, no clear plan. I think about equal days and nights, balance, making things even.

My refrigerator survey reveals spinach in the bottom vegetable drawer, the marrow bone from a pot roast, and half a package of fresh pasta. In the freezer I find a ham hock, some tomatoes, and a handful of peas from the summer's garden. The last Walla Walla sweet onion sits on the counter. It's time to clean out the stores by making something good to eat.

I begin with the ham hock and the marrow bone and put them to boil with the onion and a couple of garlic cloves. I go to work at my computer while the ingredients of the broth simmer. An hour or so later, I strain the broth and add the frozen tomatoes and chopped spinach. There are two slightly dry carrots in the fridge, and these go into the soup too. I pull bits of ham off the hock and drop them back into the mixture.

By now I am patting myself on the back for being well on the way to good homemade minestrone. I go back to my computer, taking breaks now and then to add different ingredients: a sprinkling of oregano, a clipping of parsley from the pot by the kitchen door, a small can of red beans from the pantry shelf, a handful of the frozen garden peas. The savory smell of broth rises, along with the scent of homegrown tomatoes, as I clean out my refrigerator and make soup for dinner. Hurray for the equinox.

The day goes on. I've finished grading papers from my Irish literature class. I've taken the dogs for a walk through the little oak woods, enjoying the yellow September light. I've gone in and out several times to stretch my legs after working at the computer, and I've talked on the phone to one of my sisters and one of my daughters. I have a pleasant feeling of balance, in sympathy with the earth's turning around the sun. I feel like a minor goddess. Late in the afternoon, I add a handful of pasta to the soup, which smells delicious. I wander to the living room where my husband is watching football. I go outside to look at the real world and take a meander down the pasture.

As I reenter the house, there is something not right in the air. I smell scorching food. The soup, turned low, was not low enough. I pour it into another kettle to inspect the damage. The bottom of the pan is blackened. I taste the soup. Like ashes.

Shall I cry? Swear? Serve it and see if my husband notices? I let the soup cool on the countertop. I go back to my computer and read e-mail. When the soup is cool enough, I take it out to the chickens and toss it into the pen. They are delighted, dragging the strings of pasta out of the glop, pecking at the vegetables. To the chickens, I am always a gourmet cook. What they don't eat drains into the earth, an equinoctial sacrifice.

Back in the house I scramble eggs for sandwiches—eggs from our chickens that are enjoying the soup. I find some chives in the garden and chop them onto the eggs. I spoon the eggs onto toast and grind pepper onto the eggs. Then I butter two more pieces of toast and put these lids on the sandwiches. I pour two glasses of pinot noir from our small vineyard and take the sandwiches and wine to the living room.

"What happened to the soup?" asks my husband.

"Don't ask," I say.

He is a nice husband. He doesn't ask again.

We eat our scrambled egg sandwiches and sip pinot. The refrigerator is a little less cluttered. My papers are graded. The chickens are fed and amused. Day and night balance in the scale of the universe. I ponder the long tradition of burnt offerings.

Autumn begins.

Bonfire

It's Thursday again, already a week after Thanksgiving, and Bill and I are finally getting around to cleaning house. The vacuum cleaner sits at the far end of the living room where one of us dropped it after making a half-hearted attempt to sweep up when guests had gone. The site of the bonfire above the vineyard is a sodden, gray, ashy ruin after a week of rain, and last night there was a dusting of snow. We were lucky this year. Thanksgiving Day was dry with patches of sun between high-flying clouds. Sometimes Thanksgiving is too wet for a fire, though we always give it a try.

The bonfire started with a seven-foot-high pile of grape cuttings from the vineyard, saved from the previous year. Mobs of grandchildren, like kindergarten revolutionaries, charged up the hill with sticks in their hands aiming to feed the fire. My Thanksgiving gratitude centered on the fact that no one burned their fingers, and also that it didn't rain, so we were able to accommodate, both indoors and out, forty-five-plus family members and friends.

Our house is not large, and the bonfire encouraged people to drift in and out. The grown-up nephews and brothers-in-law stood around drinking beer and now and then poking at the hot coals with a long stick. The little kids, normally not allowed to play with fire, suddenly found themselves with not only the savage urge but also permission to toss flammable objects into the glowing heart of the coals. Besides the grape cuttings, we fed the blaze with chunks of rotten wood from a long-fallen barn and pieces of oak too tough and twisted to be split for the indoor stove.

I was afraid we wouldn't be able to get a fire going this year, it had been so wet, but in view of tradition and my fervent desire to have a bonfire, Bill took the propane torch and shot flames into the pile of cuttings and wet wood. We all stared as he turned up the heat repeatedly with no effect, but suddenly the propane blast caught and started the fire with an exciting roar that spoke to the heart of the family pyromaniacs. And burn it did, with flames ten feet tall and a ring of heat that made the cold weather seem like summer at the beach. After ten minutes we had a warm spot in the dark day, and it would last into the night.

Even my mother, over ninety years old, went out in the damp to celebrate by the fire. She sat in one of the camp chairs while the great grandchildren came and went, leaned on her shoulder and stared into the heat as the adults laughed and told stories and sipped their beer, Jim Beam, or wine from our vineyard.

Meanwhile, the party continued inside the house. One niece had just announced her engagement, so she and her fiancé moved among relatives with the newly acquired status of a young about-to-be-married couple. Our children and their spouses arrived. Twelve grandchildren were here, including the youngest, who had just arrived from Alaska. The nieces and nephews had also brought friends who were either far from home or had simply chosen a country Thanksgiving over whatever else was going on in their lives. It had been cold all week, and there was a frost the night before, but the bonfire, along with the bright sun that lit up the last of the yellow leaves on the grape vines, held us together in the out-of-doors.

For two days I'd been worrying that there wouldn't be enough food, but with no cause—as usual, the food was abundant. I'd prepared the traditional turkey, dressing, potatoes and gravy, along with four pies and a pan full of baked squash from our garden. Mom brought her own complement of pies, lemon and apple. My sisters showed up with baskets full of ham and salads and drinks. The kids brought various side dishes and snacks, from caviar and cheese dip to bean salad and dolmathes. The problem was not too little food, but too little available space. Somehow we arranged it all on the three kitchen tables and the old cherry harvest table in the living room. Bill had brought in the wine that morning. The next day he would count the empty bottles, not because he had wished to save them, but with pleasure that people had enjoyed his homemade pinot noir from our vineyard.

Now this year's Thanksgiving was receding into the past, though I continued to be thankful. What is it about such a gathering that always makes it work? The people, of course, and the food and the tradition. But also the bonfire. And what is it about a bonfire that makes the event?

Some sources say the word bonfire is a version of bonefire or that the seasonal bonfires of Easter, midsummer night, and Halloween or November, are based on ancient European pagan ceremonies. Some associations of a bonfire are dark, suggesting witchcraft, executions, or destruction. Whether these associations are true or not, I would also like to think the word could be read as bon, or good, a good fire. Our bonfires are happy events, warming us when the fall season is turning toward dark and rain, or lighting the way at Easter when we are coming out of the cold and dark. It is a spectacle and a warm hearth, as it turns faces pink and smokes the air with a scent of old wood and grape cuttings. Both the autumn and the spring bonfires create a natural transition and a purifying ritual that allow us to burn the debris of the fall cleaning and winter pruning.

When I was a child, before mulch became a byword of modern environmentalism, we burned raked-up leaves in the fall, and it is a smell I will never forget: tangy, sour, and earthy, a smoky spice and a pungent taste, an incense I still love. Nowadays people are encouraged to mulch their yard debris or to have it collected by an enlightened city sanitary service, which will turn the old summer detritus into rich humus and topping for gardens. Especially in areas where the land forms a basin and the fires of wood stoves pollute the air during a temperature inversion, the bonfire is a retrograde and un-ecological event. But on our breezy hilltop, twice yearly, we indulge in this cleansing, outdoor fire.

When we first moved to the country, leaving a densely popu-lated and constantly lit city neighborhood, I loved the peace of the rural landscape and the long sunlit days. As fall came on, though, I sometimes felt a certain sadness or melancholy when I drove home from work and turned onto our little country road; it was very dark out. In the city I rarely thought about darkness. In fact the city was never truly dark. In the country, as Christmas came and people on the distant hills and in houses down the road began to hang Christ-mas lights, I was surprised that it made me feel happy to see these lights spotted throughout the dark landscape. There was a feeling of joy, a lifting of spirits at seeing the Christmas lights. I had never noticed this feeling in Portland, where light was constant and every-where and too many multi-colored strands of bulbs seemed garish and commercial. I was not a bah-humbug sort of person, but once I became an adult, bright Christmas lights in the city barely scratched my emotional surface. They were just part of the general celebration and holiday sales campaign.

We had lived in the country for a year and a half—it was our second country Christmas—when I identified the source of that lifting of spirits that had been oh-so-slightly but definitely subdued by the seasonal darkness. Again Christmas lights began to appear on people's distant houses. Again light in the darkness felt good.

One evening I was driving home from work and saw a glow and a haze of smoke over a neighbor's field. A stack of baled straw, the leavings of a grass seed harvest, had been sitting in the field through-out the fall. This was no small amount of straw. It was an enormous shoebox-shaped pile of straw bales the size of a boxcar. Either the wet, decaying bales had started to burn on their own, or the farmer had lit them to get rid of them before it was time to plant his field again. This was over twenty years ago. Nowadays there is an export market for straw. Other countries use it for paper or, with the addition of certain nutrients and various unsavory but apparently usable ingredients, turn it into cattle feed where grazing land is scarce. But in the year when the enormous straw pile burned this was not the case. Straw, left over from the wheat or grass seed harvest, sold for less than fifty cents a bale that year, and it was not worth the gas and effort for farmers to take it anywhere else. What they could not sell or use for animal bedding they burned in the field. That enormous pile of straw became an enormous bonfire.

I know I am exaggerating, but in memory it feels as if the straw pile burned from Thanksgiving till Christmas. As the days became shorter and shorter, it made a sweet, hot light in the dark. I realized I had a primeval need for light. Sometimes in the dark days I still yearn for it.

This is not to say that I enjoy light pollution. I have learned to love the soft blackness of a clear night when the moon is dark, and I can go out in our field with my little telescope to look for Saturn, Jupiter, and Venus. There is something about extreme darkness that is as satisfying as a black, velvet cape draped on the shoulders.

This year, at the family Thanksgiving picnic, as dark came on, people continued to stand around the bonfire. It got colder and colder and slowly the spent fuel dwindled into a pile of sparkling fire snakes crawling in the ash. People began to leave the fire and went indoors, but I could not bear to think of the outdoor spectacle ending, so I asked if anyone wanted to take a walk through the woods. Several of the children were up for it, and some of the other relatives were too, including my ex-husband, the father of my children, who was among the guests. Bill elected to stay at the house, to start bringing order to the kitchen. The night-walkers took a minimal number of flashlights in order to prevent falls over tree roots, and about a dozen of us proceeded through the dark along the driveway and into the south oak woods.

My son had received a new GPS device for his birthday, so he set it—not to keep us from getting lost, since the way through the woods was more than familiar, and I, at least, might have been able to walk it with my eyes closed—but to play with his new toy and measure the distance we traveled.

One six-year-old granddaughter, who had commandeered a flashlight, turned back before we went into the woods. She lives in the city, and perhaps her courage failed her at the last minute, faced with so much darkness, or perhaps she just had to go to the bathroom. In any case, she turned and ran back to the house. The rest of us, along with the dogs, plunged into the woods, following the path that had been defined by sheep, deer, our own feet, and from time to time, the mower. We now had only two small flashlights, but somehow the dark seemed to wrap around and support us in the alley of closely packed oaks.

We walked slowly along the path to the bottom of the woods, then out into the little clearing with the wild apple trees and a scattering of two-year old pines, then on into the darkest woods of all, where the bare branches of ash trees and wild cherries, pears, apples, and plums supported thick swags of blackberry vines and wild rose brambles, a dank fairytale bog of vegetation and mud. We went up the hill into the little pasture, through the tangled hedge into the clearing at the bottom of the vineyard, and finally between the pinot noir and the chardonnay plantings, back to the bonfire. The air was sweet and clean and cold in the dark.

My ex was cautious, not having walked this way before, but it was fun to see him in the midst of the grandchildren. I had three-year-old Mavis by the hand, though she would have liked to run wildly as she had been doing much of the afternoon through the daylight hours. When we had circled around and arrived back at the bonfire, half a dozen celebrants were still warming themselves, though there was little light coming from the ashes by now. Later, my son Moss checked his GPS readings on the computer and proclaimed that we had walked .5 miles, not so far. Still, we returned to the house triumphant. Darkness and light. We needed both. In having made our way through the dark woods and back into the light, we had fortified ourselves for the coming of winter.

Grandmother Trees

A woman who signed up to take one of my writing classes caused me to think about the various connections people feel to places. We were working on writing about family when she revealed that her grandmother had once lived on a farm near ours. I recognized the farm she described, as well as the line of evergreens that she told me her grandmother had planted long ago for a windbreak and a source of shade. Bill and I pass that line of trees almost every day when we take our dogs for a morning walk.

The farm where her grandmother lived is on a west-facing slope. The place was for sale at the time we were looking for a farm, and a realtor sent us out to look at it. It didn't suit us—no woods, a manufactured home, too open—but it was this exploratory trip that led us to spot a weathered For Sale sign on the place we did end up buying. The other farm was on a nice piece of land, though. It was twenty acres, had a view of the Coast Range, and the line of big old fir trees on the north side caught my attention.

The woman in my class went on to describe how, as a little girl, she saw her grandmother planting and hand-watering the little trees. Through more than one hot summer, the grandmother carried bucket after bucket of water to the long row of baby trees until they finally had enough of a root system to survive on their own. I wonder if the people who live there now, some fifty years later, have ever thought about who might have planted that line of evergreens.

On our morning walks, we wave at the people who live there if they drive past in their truck. Someday, if I see someone out in the yard, I should tell them the story of their trees—though it's not my story, and I'm not sure of the details.

We have planted and rearranged some things on our farm since we moved here many years ago. The world is an accumulation of such efforts. I hope that future residents will like the things we have done. When I look over our place, and many of the other places in the world where there are landscapes that nurture, comfort, and satisfy, I give thanks to the unknown elders who bothered to plant and water, tend and preserve, often struggling with the constraints of wind and weather, water shortage and physical effort. The tall, sixty-foot-long lilac hedge on the south side of our house is one such gift. The lilacs seem very old; they were probably planted by the same family who brought us the cistern. Each spring, when sweet-smelling lilac blossoms burst forth on the high old branches, I say a little prayer of appreciation.

I enjoyed working with the student who told me about her grandmother and the trees. She was a cheerful, rambunctious lady, a wife and mother who liked big pickups and had strong opinions. We exchanged stories about the area. Once in a while I would mention having walked by her grandmother's old place.

One time I told her about the horned owls that fly out of our woods at night in the direction of her grandmother's fields, and when the class ended she gave me a generous gift, a little brass figure of an owl, about two inches high. It had come to her from her grandmother. I keep it on the shelf above my desk in honor of owls, trees, and grandmothers.

Nature and Nurture

❖

I congratulate myself. Today I pruned a rose bush. Three rose bushes in fact. But in spite of enjoying the country life, I'm not much of a gardener. I have an instinct against pruning. If Bill is clearing brush to keep the pasture under control, I feel grateful for his hard work, but I also feel a kind of irrational pissed-off-ness if he cuts back too much of a wild rose. I love the way these wild plants climb up fences and fruit trees, build trellises out of their old canes, and then spill back down in a waterfall of blossoms, the leaves changing color from pale yellow-green early in spring to deep green in summer and finally to rust-rimmed gold in the fall. Out of control—and that's the way I like them.

I realize that my own gardening doesn't always show well to visitors. The whole twenty acres has so much beauty, but the flower gardens around the house are sketchy at best. For one thing, there's the limited well water. I make a modest attempt to cultivate and nurture plants that will look pretty and provide flowers and foliage through the growing season, and I plant a few things that provide bouquets, but nothing that requires a lot of irrigation. We save water for the vegetable garden.

When we first moved here we put in some foundation shrubs around the house, and every year or two I drop more daffodil and tulip bulbs in the ground—ignoring them till spring. I put easy plants like geraniums, snapdragons, petunias, lobelia, fuchsias, and succulents in pots around the house—a little color here, a little greenery there. But I have to choose where to spend time and water, and by and large, I believe that the most beautiful landscapes are the ones created by nature.

Our place isn't exactly wild, since we try to keep blackberries and scotch broom from taking over, and Bill uses the tractor to keep a trail clear through the woods, but a lot of it is pretty wild.

At the front of our property the narrow oak woods are about forty or fifty feet deep and seven hundred feet long. These oaks are crowded and create a tangle compared to the freestanding, mushroom-shaped, centuries-old oaks. The smaller trees support a thick growth of lush, bright, green mosses, silvery or greenish staghorn lichens, seaweed-like lungworts, and numerous other life forms. Among the lichens, the lungworts especially fascinate me. I was confused when I first tried to identify them because the name also refers to a flowering plant in the borage family. But the lungwort on our place is a macrolichen.

Depending on the season, our lungworts are brownish-black on one side and dry and pasty on the other, or electric green on one side and creamy white on the other. Hot summer dry-crackling or wet winter lush-and-leathery, the lungworts take advantage of the leafless canopy and moisture to flourish in wet months and withdraw in a muted survival state in the dark shade of leafy oaks in summer drought. Lungworts, like other lichens, are a fascinating dual entity, a symbiotic combination of a fungus and photosynthesizing algae growing within the fungus. To me, an amateur naturalist with an all-too-skimpy background in science, lichens are an evolutionary creation I am still trying to get my head around. But even if I only partially understand them, I am especially happy about all the lichens that grow well here because they are an indicator of clean air.

Lichens are also pretty to look at. At any time of year, the bark of the oaks together with the various textures and forms of mosses, fungus, and lichens create a beautiful display of light and dark, sun and shade, linear forms and soft coverings, all without the efforts of a gardener. The ground underneath the trees is similarly beautiful, its character depending on seasonal weather and light conditions. There are ferns, mushrooms, fallen leaves, the invasive yet lovely little wild geraniums of spring, and an understory of wild rose, Indian plum, wild cherry, and snowberry bushes. In some places luxuriant mosses also grow on the ground, forming soft beds six inches deep or more.

The peak of the natural display may be in early April, when the ground beneath the oaks is covered with hundreds of *Erythronium*, also known as dogtooth violets or fawn lilies. The recurved and pointed petals of these perennials bend back with the grace of floral ballerinas, and the leaves, dappled in reddish and green tints, imitate the pattern of light and shadow coming through the partially leafed-out oaks.

The more neglect, it seems, the more variety in the flowerings. Once in a while we bring home seeds from other wildflowers in our general area. This might account for the fact that three years ago a pink *Erythronium,* also known as a trout lily, appeared among the yellow *Erythronium* in our woods. Now there is a small but increasing patch of the pink variety. A few years ago, we also noticed some brown and creamy, yellow checker lilies or fritillaries, growing in several spots. Had they been carried in somehow or were they simply recovering and coming back after the years when we let sheep browse in the woods?

Later, in May, the wild roses bloom in varied shades of pink and white along the fence at the forest's edge, and thereafter until the end of summer there is a succession of various wildflowers on the place.

One of the beautiful but not-so-welcome native wild plants on the place is poison oak. In fall, the leaves turn red and make a showy accent in the autumn landscape. Sheep eat it without experiencing apparent harm, but where it leans over into the footpaths one must use gloves, clippers, and occasionally the tractor to clear the plant from human trails. There's no way to get rid of it completely.

For the most part, the woodland takes care of itself, occasionally dropping limbs we gather for firewood. Sometimes a small tree dies as others crowd and overtop it as the young forest makes slow progress toward mature oak woodland. In autumn, abundant fallen leaves carpet the forest and return their nourishment to the soil. Walking through the woods at this time of year, I think of that grand line by Victorian poet Alfred Lord Tennyson: "The woods decay, the woods decay and fall." And so they do.

It is not only the woods that have this natural loveliness, but our fields do as well. The old fields have been browsed but only rarely mowed, and the remains of cultivated and wild grasses and clovers have mixed with *Sisyrinchium* or blue-eyed grass, Queen Anne's lace, pale-blue wild flax, pink checkermallows, wild onions, purplish-blue harvest brodiaea, and lavender-blue ookow, also known as blue dicks. In late spring, on the lower, wetter parts of the property, there are patches of blue camas flowers, and near the road a few plants of the white death camas grow, looking to me a little like a smaller bear grass. There used to be orange columbines on the east edge of the property, but they disappeared after the county graded the roadside.

As summer goes on, the sky-blue flowers of wild chicory glow in the light. A relative of the salad green radicchio, chicory flowers have a clock-like punctuality, usually closing after noon. Wild irises grow along the fence in the upper woods, and in the west pasture there are yellow-flowered lomatium (*Lomatium nudicaule*), on which we have sometimes seen swallowtail larvae browsing. Recently we were surprised to find pink shooting stars in the upper woods where we had never seen them before, though browsing deer made short work of the blossoms, which would explain their scarcity. In a couple of spots there are even tiny but persistent patches of lady's tresses, a creamy white orchid, and striped coralroot, another orchid.

Such is the flower garden of neglect.

The drawback to wild gardens, of course, is their seasonal nature. In the hot, dry months of late summer, flowering is sparse except for Queen Anne's lace, which has blossoms that float like beautiful white doilies above the drying grass. This beautiful plant turns annoying when it goes to seed, and its tiny burrs attach to the dogs' fur and my socks.

Some other gardeners prize a natural look. The Japanese and Chinese Gardens in Portland and The Oregon Garden near Silverton, with its water gardens and various themed plantings, are so beautiful it is a spiritual act to visit them. And yet these natural look-ing gardens, which sometimes imitate what nature does on its own, require much labor and tending. The stones, the sand, the twisted trees, the elegant pines, and the rustling bamboo, were all arranged by someone with greater artistic vision and more labor and money than I can muster. Our vegetable garden necessarily gets most of our water from the drip irrigation system hooked up to the old well at the top of the hill. The pots and small spaces around the house where I have planted my geraniums, snapdragons, lavender, and oth-er easily tended plants that love heat and attract hummingbirds, get stored rainwater from the old cistern, which we draw with the hand pump into a watering can.

The seeding grasses ripen after most of the wildflowers, and they are varied and lovely. If only grasses could satisfy my wish for flowering, all would be easy, but as the wildflowers pass, I want a few flowers near the house, so I deadhead my leggy roses and my little plot of snapdragons to keep them going, and plant chrysanthemums and over-wintering pansies in pots to make fall color.

The pots around the house look pretty, and hummingbirds visit all day long. The roses can stand one more pruning before I leave them to put on rose hips and retire for fall. All of these plantings are lovely, and yet nothing, I will say it again, nothing, seems quite as good or as beautiful as the natural displays in the neglected pastures and woods of our old farm, where the plants run their own wild show.

Though I celebrate the natural abundance of beautiful wild-flowers on our farm, a visitor to our place might miss it. One would never see a whole field with all of these flowers at once, because each has its time in the annual succession. The *Erythronium,* or fawn lily, flourishes mostly in the shade-and-sunshine mix of the oak trees before they have fully leafed out in April. There may be two or three hundred of these lilies blooming for about three weeks in the spring. Though they sometimes venture to the edge of the woods, we never find them in the open pasture. This is also true of the pink fawn lilies and the checkerlilies, which are fairly scarce in numbers. The blue camas flowers tend to be in low-lying wet places, and bloom a little later than the fawn lilies and the other woodland flowers, but they too stay in places most hospitable to their needs.

Some wildflowers, such as the yellow, daisy-like Oregon sunshine, were a surprise to us in recent years. So far this newcomer exists only in a tiny space, perhaps no bigger than a foot square, at the roadside edge of the pasture.

The purple wild irises are scattered in the upper oak woods. There are more irises than there are shooting stars, which occur only in two small areas, but neither is abundant.

Of the orchids, the lady's tresses and the striped coralroot, we usually only find a very few each year, maybe five or six, maybe only one or two, depending on the past year's weather or browsing deer or some cyclical whim of the plants.

The lovely, blue harvest brodiaea, which appear in July when the field grass turns to a warm, almost pink, straw color, have become much more abundant since we quit letting sheep into that part of the field, and so has the white brodiaea, or fool's onion. Both of these are lilies that can propagate by bulblets. There were always so many gopher mounds in that area, we were afraid that the gophers might be eating and destroying the plants, but after a few years of observation, I wonder if the opposite might be true. Even if they eat some of the bulbs, the gophers might be spreading them by consuming the main bulb and leaving behind the small bulblets. Some years the flowers actually seem to be more abundant and dispersed in the area of gopher mounds.

Perhaps this is just wishful thinking. In any case, except for the *Erythronium* and the widespread chicory and Queen Anne's lace, nowhere is there a dense and widespread showing of any one variety of wildflower at one time, and because the different flowers bloom in a staggered schedule, rather than all at once, there is never anything like the dense flowering of a cultivated garden.

My point is that even though the list of wildflowers on our place seems long to me, the flowers themselves are rare and delicate. They seem to thrive best when they are left alone. There are other magnificent wildflowers nearby, such as the calypso orchids that grow in hillside colonies in the undisturbed woods surrounding nearby Hagg Lake. Human activity there mostly centers on boating, swimming, and fishing, while the woods are left to a few hikers or to mountain bikers, who tear down the center of the trails and move too quickly to linger over hillsides of tiny orchids. I doubt whether most of the speeding mountain bikers ever even see the calypsos, with their little dragon-like heads, deep pink petals, and speckled throats.

I would love to have calypso orchids on our place, but it's against the law to dig plants in the park, and even if it weren't, their delicate root structure makes them virtually impossible to transplant. Some wildflower seeds are easy to collect, such as camas or columbine, but orchid seeds are microscopic. One online reference says it takes 416,992 calypso seeds to make a pound. Give or take a few? Besides being tiny, the seeds need the right mycorrhizal companions in the soil to grow. I wonder, if I simply scraped up a handful of dirt from the slopes where the calypsos grow, and scattered the dirt in our woods, might the dirt contain seed and mychorrhizae enough that the orchid would one day appear on our place? I might try it. Surely no one could object to my taking a handful of dirt home in my pocket. In the meantime, it's exciting when we find coralroot or lady's tresses on our own place. An orchid is an orchid.

The delicate balance that just the right habitat provides is so important to wildflowers, and timing is part of that balance. When a roadside mowing crew chooses to cut back blackberry vines during the flowering of wild camas, as they did on our road this past spring, not only is the camas display spoiled, but the fruits don't have a chance to ripen and drop seeds for future years.

Lupine is a fairly common wildflower in this area. Lupine is not usually an endangered plant, but the Kincaid's lupine grows only sparsely and is host to the endangered Fender's blue butterfly. Now the plant itself has become scarce. This past summer, on behalf of our local chapter of the Native Plant Society of Oregon, Bill volunteered to monitor a few Kincaid lupine sites in the hills west of us to make sure that no one was spraying or mowing there. When he went out to check them, I went along. We saw the county's recently posted signs banning spraying or mowing of the lupine. The roadside patches were small and isolated, but this year at least no one had mown or sprayed them.

Why do wild things matter enough that we should protect them? I am almost tempted to ignore this question since wildflowers, creatures, lichens, ferns, and even the tiny unknown organisms in the dirt are their own reason for being. Each is unique and wonderful in its own right. But scientists who know more about these things than I do assure us there is a network of dependencies in nature. If Fender's blue butterfly depends on Kincaid's lupine, who knows what depends on the Fender's blue?

Poison Oak

Poison oak is a native plant throughout the grasslands and oak forests of Yamhill County. Native or not, it's my enemy—as are other urushiol-containing plants, such as poison ivy or poison sumac—and it has been since I was ten years old. So I don't know why I didn't realize our farm was poison oak habitat until after we bought the place and moved here. We would have bought the place anyway, but my experience with the allergenic plant should have immediately come to mind.

When I was a child, to stand on the edge of woodland was to hover in an eddy of attraction, like a paper boat on the lip of a falls. One hesitant moment, and then I was off: following deer trails, climbing trees, traversing mossy gullies on fallen logs, discovering, in short, what was there.

Naturally the woods behind the house in Camas, Washington, where I lived briefly during grade school, exerted a strong pull. But not long after any trip into that forest, I found myself itching with a rash that soon formed blisters. My enchanting woods were infested with poison oak.

If my dog chased a rabbit into the woods, and I later embraced him, I broke out in a rash. If I brushed some roadside weeds on my way to and from the school bus, I would soon be covered in oozing red spots. It seemed I had only to walk a foot or two into the woods to have a reaction. Sometimes it seemed that if I so much as breathed the country air I would break out in blisters.

My mother was frantic in her attempts to keep me whole and uninfected. "Don't go into the woods anymore," she directed. "Do you hear me?" She said this with such a stern, imploring tone that I tried to mind her, and yet I could not resist the call. I would stay out of the forest until my poison oak had cleared, but then one day I would find myself hovering on the edge of the trees, peering into the shadows. Suddenly, overcome with a desire for wildness, my dog and I would dash along a winding deer trail to the top of the ridge and back, as if by traveling quickly the toxic oils of the plant would not catch me.

In a matter of days, I would again look like a ten-year-old leper with running sores, swollen eyes, and the smell of calamine emanating from my inflamed skin.

Little water bubbles would form on my skin like grease simmering in a hot pan. When one bubble burst, and its fluid dribbled downward, soon there would appear another line of bubbles, each one smaller than the preceding one. This led me to think that the fluid from the first blister must have received the most toxic dose of the poison, the second less, and so on, until the dwindling amount of poison created the smallest, bottom-most bubble. I have been told by doctors that poison oak cannot spread in this way, but experience tells me otherwise. Somehow the fluid in the blisters managed to spread the toxin that must have bonded inseparably to my skin. It seemed as though the poison oak had regenerated within me, and that my own body was producing the vile fluid that caused my skin to redden, itch, and erupt in this revolting and uncomfortable way. Catching it from myself in this way was highly depressing.

People were generous in suggesting half-assed remedies to my mother. Make a poison oak tea. (Happily, she didn't.) Bathe in laundry soap. (A drying and irritating effect.) Don't wash the infection at all—water makes it spread. (The result was skin covered by a caked, plaster-like layer of grimy calamine, decorated with dried and crystallized fluid that had seeped from broken blisters.) Soaking in bathwater containing generous amounts of baking soda was another suggestion and this offered some relief from itching, at least while I stayed in the water, and also had the good effect of washing off the caked calamine, but in the end washing after the reaction had begun did not cure anything.

None of these homemade solutions worked, and one day after a detergent bath my skin took on a hardened, red quality. It was then that the worst consequence of the poison oak appeared. I woke in the morning with a high fever and throbbing, baseball-sized lumps under my right armpit and in the groin. Red streaks climbed both my leg and my arm. My parents took me to a doctor, who proclaimed I had blood poisoning. I lay on the surgeon's table as, with a wooden spatula, he scraped raw the now-bubbling, white, and fungus-like surface of the skin that covered my right hand and the back of my right leg. I felt as if I were a hide being scraped and cured, soon to be pinned to a weathered wall like the coyote and cow skins I'd seen on rural barns.

Next the doctor applied medicine to the inflamed, open sore and then prescribed something else. It was the 1940s, before penicillin use was common, and I don't know what it might have been, sulfa perhaps. When he was finished, the flesh on my leg and hand had been laid bare, and the raw surface throbbed like a burn.

For days I had to lie on my stomach, my arms outstretched, as my mother applied sterile gauze soaked in some sort of disinfecting liquid calculated to draw out the poison. Whatever the medicines were, the cure took a long time. My hand and leg throbbed unbearably as I lay face down, tears dripping onto my pillow, trying to distract myself by listening to radio soap operas and quiz shows such as *One Man's Family* and *Queen for a Day*.

I developed a love-hate relationship with those woods, where before it was all affection.

That was a lifetime ago. Where I live now in western Oregon it's still hard to get away from poison oak anywhere outside of a city. On my Yamhill County farm, poison oak is a constant presence, though it thrives mainly in the shadows of the oak woods and along the roadside.

Poison oak can be quite beautiful, especially in the fall when it turns red and gold. Once, before we learned what it was, my mother brought an armful of the branches into the house to make an autumn bouquet. When my father saw the leaves in a vase on the dining room table, he threw the bouquet, container and all, out the door. Though my mother had gathered that bouquet she didn't "catch" it. I've read that around 15 percent of people are not sensitive to poison oak, though exposure may later make them so. Although we are accustomed to thinking of exposure as helpful to developing immunity to a substance, this is not usually the case with poison oak.

Why are some people immune to its effects and others not? Was I was exposed to too much of it at a young age and thus permanently sensitized? I've often wondered why poison oak exerts its toxic affect. Most plants that have offending characteristics benefit from them: bitterness and thorns to fend off devouring animals, burrs to spread. Yet our sheep eat the young leaves of poison oak with no apparent harm. The berries are bird food. How does the plant benefit from what it can do to people? Perhaps human allergy is just coincidence.

In the *Cascade-Olympic Natural History,* author Daniel Mathews says, "Unlike nettle stingers—an elaborate and effective defense against browsing—poison-ivy/oak/sumac poison has little survival value to the plant. Call it an accident of biochemistry, or one of the commonest allergies in *Homo sapiens.* Other species don't seem to be susceptible; they gather the nectar, or browse the leaves with pronounced indifference. In humans, susceptibility can be acquired but rarely shed." I have seen honey for sale with the label "poison oak honey." Perhaps honey gathered by bees from poison oak inflorescences appeals to people who believe in the homeopathic approach, that ingesting small amounts of the poison will render one immune to its effects. Not me. Some people today still recommend drinking tea made from the leaves, but I would never dare to do that, nor would I knowingly enter an area where someone might be burning brush containing poison oak. Mathews also says that, "There have been fatalities following poison-ivy smoke inhalation—drownings, technically, in a sea of blister fluid in the lungs. (The toxin is destroyed by complete burning, but smoke may carry unburned particles.)" If we are burning brush we are always careful not to include poison oak in the fire.

Still, people have always looked for the potential usefulness of something with no apparent use, and this is true of poison oak or poison ivy as well. I consulted my old copy of Mrs. Grieve's *A Modern Herbal,* an antique catalogue of useful plants and planted-related folklore. Mrs. Grieve wrote that in 1798 the first medicinal use of the oil of poison oak occurred in England when a Dr. Du Fressoy came across the accidental curing of a young man's "herpetic eruption" of six years by the application of the sap. Thereafter the plant was used to cure "obstinate herpetic eruptions," "palsy," "paralysis, acute rheumatism and articular stiffness, and . . . various forms of chronic and obstinate eruptive diseases," including ringworm and rashes caused by food allergies. Besides referring to treatment of eruptions and arthritis, Mrs. Grieve goes on to say that a tincture of the root bark of poison ivy taken "in wineglassful doses" may relieve incontinence of urine, and that the "milky juice" of the plant "is also used as an indelible ink for marking linen, and as an ingredient of liquid dressings or varnishes for finishing boots or shoes." Though this all sounds dubious to me, and certainly risky, I am impressed by the human-centric belief that somehow all living things might serve our good if we can only discover the means to use them.

People suffer a variety of allergies, but allergy to poison oak is especially common. I wonder if the native Kalapuyan people of this area were susceptible to it. I am accustomed to thinking of nature as benign, so long as we do not actually ingest the plants we know to be poisonous. I've read that contact with poison oak is harmless if the leaf has not been bruised to release the urushiol, so brushing a plant lightly ought to be fine, but in my experience it's not.

My unpleasant relationship with poison oak is all the more difficult since our landscape is actually defined, in part, by its presence. Our farm's soils are Willakenzie and Hazelair, soils found on the west side of the Willamette Valley in the slopes adjacent to the Coast Range. According to the United States Department of Agriculture Soil Survey for the Yamhill area, the characteristic plants of uncultivated Willakenzie-Hazelair soils are "oak trees, poison-oak, grass, and widely spaced Douglas-fir trees."

Of course, ours is not the only area where poison oak prospers. It's also common in other parts of the Willamette Valley, in the Columbia Gorge, and in many wooded places along the Oregon Coast. It is not generally found in the Cascades or the high desert of Oregon, and in my experience it doesn't show up in the higher, more exposed areas of the Coast Range either, although I'm not sure that this is a fact. Ellen Morris Bishop in her book, *In Search of Ancient Oregon,* mentions that poison oak appears in the fossil evidence of the Oligocene, in the Painted Hills on the east side of the Cascades. An ancient plant indeed.

A related plant containing the same allergen, urushiol, is poison ivy, which is more common in the eastern part of the United States. When I lived in Michigan I found it growing on fencerows, where it mingled with the charming wild fox grape, and even in the grass, where it came up as low-growing leaves. Poison oak and poison ivy, which both belong to the genus *Toxicodendron* of the family Anacardiaceae, seem to adapt to a variety of forms—shrub, vine, or groundcover—depending on the landscape. Their motto: whatever works. The allergen is not only present in the leaves but also in the roots, stems, and bare winter branches. Though the plants can always cause a reaction, they are most dangerous in the spring when the sap rises and the new leaves are tender and easily bruised.

Over the years, I've learned more or less how to deal with poison oak: Avoid it if possible. Failing that, wash immediately after accidental or possible exposure. Soaps have been developed that effectively remove the irritant from the skin. Technu brand "outdoor skin cleanser," used quickly enough, will remove the oils that cause the reaction and are said to be useful in decontaminating "laundry, pets, and tools" as well. Washing thoroughly and soon after contact with an effective cleanser is important because the irritating oil quickly bonds to the skin, followed by an allergic response within hours. Although I have read that this response can last two or three weeks, before I worked out an adequate treatment system I sometimes experienced reactions that persisted for even longer. My body seemed hysterical in its reaction against poison oak without the intervention of strong medicine.

At times when I had a particularly intractable case of poison oak, my doctors prescribed prednisone, an oral corticosteroid. This happened one summer when I was away from home, teaching a summer writing workshop at the University of Washington, and broke out with a small patch of poison oak on one eyelid the day the class began. Thin-skinned areas of the body are more susceptible to the allergy. My eyelid swelled and closed. It was awkward, to say the least, to be teaching a workshop to strangers while exhibiting this distraction. I called my doctor at home and began a course of prednisone, a large dose the first day, tapering off over a few days, and gradually the reaction subsided.

The other medication a doctor once prescribed is desoximetasone cream, described as "a high potency corticosteroid." The cream is applied to the affected area but it is not suitable for delicate skin such as around the eyes, nor should it be used unless absolutely necessary. Cautions include avoiding sun exposure and not using the medicine excessively or over a long time because it can be absorbed into the bloodstream and cause a variety of changes in body chemistry, including effects on the liver and kidneys.

In my online searches for information on poison oak and poison ivy, I came across only one lighthearted association for the plants: a site listed as the "Poison Oak and Ivy Translation Project Consortium" originating in "a harmless experiment on the walls of a bathroom stall" at Berkeley. A famous folk saying traditionally used to warn people away from poison oak and poison ivy is "Leaves of three / Leave them be." The Translation Project turned this into a language game, inviting people to see how many ways they could translate the spirit of this saying into various languages. The translations were not required to be literal, but rather to express the idea in a rhyming couplet consistent with the language used, thus: Liz Harris's French "Feuilles trois / Partez du bois!" ("Three leaves / Get out of the woods!"); someone named Jed's ancient Greek version, "trispoikiloîon / oudèn geloîon" ("Thrice-shiny thing / nothing to laugh at"); and Luigi Battizatto's Italian "terza foglia / non ho voglia," ("Three leaves, / I don't want it").

Getting rid of the plants is almost impossible. Herbicides used to kill them will kill other plants in your yard as well. Repeated cultivation of ground where poison ivy is growing may eventually get rid of the plants, but the roots need to be broken up multiple times to prevent them from regenerating. Since the plants can adapt to a variety of conditions, climbing trees or fences, spreading out in short shrubs, or just sprouting in the grass, they are very persistent.

Bill has valiantly battled the poison oak on our farm over the years, mowing it with the tractor, chopping off and pulling out long vines that climb the oak trees, and making tractor trails through the woods that let us avoid it. He too has had outbreaks, but by scrubbing with Technu soap soon after contact and treating any itchy spots with the old favorite calamine and its newer, more effective versions, he has kept them to a minimum.

After years of living here, where poison oak is common, it seems that I have become less prone to outbreaks even in spring. I wonder if this means that by not "catching it" over a long period of time I have become somewhat less sensitive to the plant's oils. Maybe older skin is less sensitive. Is that possible? It would be nice to think so, but perhaps I have just gotten better at spotting and avoiding the plant.

The lovely, seductive woods on the north side of the Colum-bia River where I first fought my battle with poison oak is now a cleared hillside covered with houses and condominiums, within the suburbs of Camas, Washington. Our rented house was torn down long ago, the woods logged, my sweet little dog given to neighbors when my parents moved us to another town and a rental where dogs were not allowed. When I drive by that place, no landmark gives me even a clue as to where I played in that forest. And yet, I suspect that even with urbanization there must be places where poison oak lies underground like an apocalyptic beast, waiting to reemerge when all else is in ruin.

Country Business

❖

All over Yamhill County there are large and small rural businesses—
the mushroom farm at the end of our road; the guy who sells garden
mulch and also makes beautiful copper stills for creating ethanol
fuel; the small blueberry farm at the edge of Carlton; not to mention
the dozens of large and small boutique wineries. There are big farms
growing wheat, alfalfa, and grass for hay or seed, people raising
livestock, artists working in home studios, beekeepers collecting
honey, and gardeners selling produce and vegetable starts from their
backyards or at farmers' markets. Hand-lettered signs at the ends of
driveways advertise "Brown eggs for sale." Many people also have
jobs elsewhere, but all of them blend their personal lives with their
country businesses.

I was curious about a CSA farm and store I passed each day on
my way to work. CSA stands for Community Supported Agriculture, and its farms are usually small and organic, catering to the local
food movement and to buyers who want to know where their food
comes from and how it was raised. Such farms usually sell shares,
offering a weekly allotment of vegetables or other products to subscribers. They also sell goods through local farmers' markets and
selected groceries and restaurants.

In addition to produce, the CSA farm near our place offered an
impressive variety of organic, locally raised meats and other farm
products. It sometimes sponsored classes. When I saw in the farm's
online newsletter that a class on making cheddar cheese was offered,
I immediately sent a message asking to be added to the list.

We were on our way out of town for a long weekend at the
coast, and I planned to drop off a check for the class when we

returned. The store was advertised as open until five, and it was a quarter to five when Bill and I pulled into the parking lot. At the back of the large house I saw a room with an open door and peered through the screen. "Hello?" I called out. No one was there.

I walked around to the door that appeared to go to the living quarters of the house and knocked. No one answered. I put my check back in my purse and left.

The next day I was out again, and on the way home I stopped at the farm. Once again the back door was mysteriously open. I opened the screen and tiptoed in. I saw a sparkling clean room with a fully furnished kitchen, some refrigerators, a cooler with gallon jars of milk, and shelves with various supplies. I felt uncomfortable about entering an empty shop, so once again I went around to the other door and knocked. A young-looking, red-haired woman appeared and led me through the house and back to the shop part of the building.

"The front is our residential area," she explained. "The shop is always open, and it's self-service."

When she said this, I realized the open door was not accidental. Customers were expected to go on in and help themselves. The owner quickly went over the details of how to take products and leave checks or money. She showed me a cooler with fresh chickens that had been butchered earlier that day and were now cooling. These organic, free-range chickens were more expensive than the ones found in supermarkets supplied by industrial farms, but having raised our own lambs and poultry, I knew how much it costs in time and resources to raise organic, healthy livestock. As I scanned the contents of the cooler, a one-pound carton of chicken livers for only $3.50 caught my eye.

A lot of people don't appreciate chicken livers. I like them floured, fried, and salted, plain or with toast, or made into pâté, but I rarely eat them because the livers of commercial chickens are usually pale, mushy, and off-putting. It seems disrespectful to waste food, so I sometimes cook those chicken livers for the dogs, and hope I'm doing the right thing. These large, meaty livers from fresh, pasture-raised chickens looked like an entirely different product, so I bought a carton. Perhaps I would make a homemade pâté. I wrote out my check for the class and the carton of livers and left, feeling a little awkward for not knowing the routine and intruding on the family living quarters. As I went out the back door of the commercial kitchen and shop, I noticed chickens running in a large fenced and grassy area and, farther back, barns with signs of other varieties of farm animals. It all looked and smelled clean, a good sign.

At home I pulled out one of the dark, red livers, floured it, and fried it in a small, lightly greased pan. I offered to cook one for Bill, but he turned me down. He says he does not eat liver, but I couldn't help but remind him that he likes liver pâté. Apparently the added butter, seasoning, and cognac make the difference.

The cooked chicken liver was good, delicate-tasting and firm. If a chicken's liver is the measure of its quality, I knew I wanted to try one of their whole chickens later.

In the meantime, I looked forward to the class and my coming enlightenment about that cheese we call cheddar.

The Saturday cheddaring class would run from one to four. I arrived about ten minutes early. Inside the shop and kitchen there were already half a dozen other participants. There was a tray of varied cheddar cheeses for tasting and a big pitcher of iced kombucha tea. I'd never tasted kombucha before, but it was thirst-quenching and pleasant. As a fermented drink, kombucha is comparable to other cultured food products, such as yogurt, kefir, kimchi, and naturally fermented sauerkraut. The health principle behind such foods is to put wholesome probiotics into your system.

I looked around. Except for the instructor, I was definitely the oldest person in the room. It didn't bother me, but I wondered if making cheese was a young person's game. The young man sitting next to me said he lived in Eugene, about two hours away, and he found out about the class online. He wanted to get into serious cheese making. A woman in front of me brought a round of her own homemade cheese. She described it as being seasoned with "jerk" spices. She hoped the cheese maker would sample and comment. Naturally cautious, I wondered about the risk of tasting experimental samples of homemade cheese made by strangers.

Many in the group were armed with their personal cheese journals recording past efforts and results, temperatures, types of milk, process, and so on. Cheese journals! I was definitely the dilettante here, though at least I had been making yogurt for over forty years, a related process. Had I written a yogurt journal, I'm afraid it would have made for dull reading.

After setting up the class and explaining that supplies were available, self-serve, in the coolers and shelves all around us, the owner of the farm and shop turned our attention to the instructor and disappeared.

The instructor was introduced as having "decades of cheese making experience," working with cow's, goat's, and sheep's milk. She had been a commercial cheese maker and was regularly the judge for the cheese-making contest at the Clark County Fair in Washington State. She was also available to answer cheese-making questions from both home and commercial cheese makers through the Clark County Extension Office. Her classes, she said, emphasized "the biochemistry of cheese making." Impressive as she was in the cheese arena, she was also surprisingly a published science fiction author—interestingly versatile. She began by explaining that cheese making, as well as yogurt making, originated mainly as a way to preserve milk, which might be seasonally overabundant at one time and scarce another.

I was so naïve about cheddar, I had expected that we would take part in a hands-on class and go home with a little chunk of cheese. How little I knew. The instructor explained that it would take at least sixty days of curing before a raw-milk cheese was considered safe to eat. This is the time required for the helpful bacteria in the cheese to overcome any potentially dangerous bacteria from the raw milk, which is preferred by many artisan cheese makers. As for taste, it might take as many as two to four years before a cheddar would be sufficiently cured to gain real distinction.

My thoughts jumped back to when I visited a small blue cheese factory on the southern Oregon coast over sixty years ago, when I was a teenager. The factory burned down long ago, sadly never to be resurrected, but I will always remember the wheels of blue cheese lined up on tall racks, in various stages of aging, from the fresh white wheels to the ones impressively furred with a deep layer of blue mold. Our guide explained that the fresh wheels were pierced and inoculated with a culture, then aged as the culture grew. When they had finished aging and before they were released, the cheese wheels were rinsed in brine that removed the fuzzy coating and left only the blue veining that made the cheese taste so distinctive. We sampled the aged cheese, and it was delicious to the point of being addictive. Even then, before I had been to France, that heaven for cheese lovers, and before I understood much about any cheese beyond Tillamook cheddar and processed Velveeta, I knew this was something I wanted to explore.

But today was about cheddar. A plate of samples allowed us to taste the range of cheeses that go by the name. The term cheddaring, I learned, described a process as much as a substance. As with blue cheeses, the cheese maker adds an appropriate culture at the beginning, as well as rennet, to get it started. In cheese making, culture is another word for helpful bacteria, of which there are many different kinds. Adding the right culture assures the consistency of the bacteria from the start.

I had my own experience with helpful bacteria, successfully making sourdough bread starter by exposing small amounts of flour and water to air and wild yeasts, gradually adding more flour and water over the days, and thereby building a live culture. When I was a graduate student at the University of Oregon, I made wine using the wild yeasts on grapes to begin fermentation. So I understood that cultures were everywhere, but I also knew that over time people preserved certain strains of choice bacteria to provide quality and consistency in whatever product was involved.

Another element in the cheese-making process, rennet, causes the milk to coagulate into curds while separating the curds from the whey. Rennet is an enzyme found in the stomach of ruminants, although there is also vegetable rennet available for vegetarians. Ancient people must have originally stored milk in bags made of animal stomachs containing the enzyme and then realized that the resultant curds offered a new type of food and a means of preservation.

As the cheese class began, there were questions from students about using raw milk and the dangers of listeria infection. Listeria is a harmful bacterium that sometimes contaminates food products such as raw milk and unpasteurized cheese and causes severe illness, potentially with long-term, debilitating effects. The instructor told the group that listeria is present everywhere, including in your sink drain. She also said she knew someone spending his life in a wheel chair due to listeria from fresh cheese at a farmer's market in Mexico. On this account, she emphasized that sanitation and care in cheese making were absolutely essential. She went on to emphasize that one should always use milk from a trustworthy supplier and follow the protocol for aging or curing the cheese. She also recommended that if a spot of mold appeared on the outside of a cheese wheel while it was aging, one should salt the spot and then clean off the mold with a touch of vinegar on a clean cloth.

I'm a fan of French raw milk cheeses and have rarely given a thought to possible problems, but now my latent food fears nudged me into thinking I would use pasteurized milk if I tried making cheese myself. My mother tells me I drank raw milk from our own Jersey cow when we lived on the farm in Kansas until I was two. I had no problems whatsoever except that our doctor said my parents should skim the milk I drank since it was so rich. But times and conditions have changed. These days I place my confidence in experienced professionals, especially the makers of French cheeses from ancient and traditional dairies and fromageries.

The instructor's knowledge was impressive. Over the next three hours she demonstrated the cheese-making process, beginning with heating two gallons of cow's milk to ninety degrees by floating a stainless steel kettle full of the milk in a large canning kettle full of hot water. She used two thermometers, one in the water and one in the milk, to assure consistency of temperature. She then added a "mesophilic starter" culture and, maintaining the temperature at ninety degrees, allowed the milk to "ripen" for thirty minutes. Next she added the rennet. The milk slowly thickened until it could be cut with a "clean break," looking more or less like soft custard. At that stage, she used a long knife to slice the custardy milk into approximately three-eighths-inch cubes by drawing the knife first one way, then the other, and then at an angle, reaching the knife into the liquid until the contents consisted of a pot of loose chunks of cultured milk. The next step was to cook the milk slowly until it reached one hundred degrees, being careful to go no higher lest the heat "shock the curd" and prevent the bacteria from working properly. She also cautioned against allowing the milk to make a "skin," and held the milk at one hundred degrees for forty-five minutes, stirring gently so as not to break the curds as they firmed and separated from the whey. There was clearly a fine balance here.

With a small pot, the instructor dipped into the mixture and slowly drew out the whey, which she poured into gallon jars. At the end of the process she told us there would be about one gallon of cheese and two and a half gallons of whey. The whey could be boiled to make another type of cheese or could be used in cooking. She told us that when she was raising her children, she mixed whey with orange juice for a drink and also used it as an ingredient in bread, pancakes, and other baking. I wondered if her children grew up to be cheese makers. Surely they were at least cheese aficionados.

The curds were drained as thoroughly as possible, using first the small pan and then a spoon. Then tipping the kettle gently to pour off the liquid, the instructor milled the curds, cutting them into half inch squares by once again sliding a knife through the contents of the pot while at the same time adding two tablespoons of salt, in three portions, allowing the salt to be absorbed slowly by the thick curds.

Now the curds went into a cloth-lined hoop, or mold, and were pressed with a cheese press. The one she used in the demonstration could be purchased or built from a plan that could also be purchased. The press was a medieval looking, hinged apparatus. Later, looking online I would see a wide variety of cheese presses. The one in class looked most like a Dutch lever cheese press. The purpose of a press was to force the cheese wheel smoothly into shape and to squeeze out extra whey, the recommended pressure being about eighty pounds for a smallish wheel.

The instructor explained that after twelve hours the cheese would be taken out of the press, the cloth peeled off, and the cheese freshly bandaged and pressed again at a heavier weight. Once the cheese had been well pressed, it would be allowed to dry at room temperature until it developed a dry rind. During this process it needed to be turned frequently to assure an even drying. After it formed a rind, it would be stored at a temperature she described as warmer than a normal refrigerator, colder than a basement. Cheddar like this could be waxed or stored in a plastic bag for aging at around forty-five degrees for three to six months, or if one wanted to be really serious about it, one to two years or longer.

As the class ended there were questions from many of the students. I wasn't sure what questions I should ask, so I just listened. Some of the others had made cheese and wanted answers as to why something didn't work the way they expected. The owner of the business came into the kitchen now and began visiting with two younger women she seemed to know. I assumed she had set up the store on a self-serve basis in order to better manage her life, but the trusting, cooperative method also seemed in keeping with the CSA philosophy. Perhaps I should mention that the couple running the CSA did not start out as farmers. Husband and wife both had backgrounds in science and engineering and had worked for a high-tech company on the outskirts of Portland. The husband still did. With a family, the farm to run, and products to market, this couple was obviously busy. I hoped everything was working well.

When I left the cheddaring class, I doubted that I would ever try making my own cheddar, but I was glad to know how it was done. I took careful notes and collected the informational handouts, but I'm sure there were still fine points I missed. I found it hard to imagine spending that much time on a wheel of cheese, which would take as long as two years to cure, when there were experienced and expert cheese makers to do it.

So I decided I would stick with the overnight process of making yogurt, either fresh or deliciously thickened by hanging it in a cheesecloth to drip overnight, Greek style. Maybe I would take a lesson from my son, who sometimes makes fresh mozzarella from pasteurized milk, which seems manageable and provides almost immediate gratification, especially served with ripe tomatoes and basil from the garden.

In any case, I love a good, ripe cheddar cheese and now have a new understanding and appreciation for it. Cheddar: a cheese. To cheddar: a verb. Let us all give thanks for makers of good cheese.

A Postscript

At the time I took the cheddaring class, the farm was selling raw milk, which many consider superior to pasteurized milk for cheese making. The wife in the partnership told me that, for quality control and other reasons, she had done all the daily milking herself, which was both time consuming and physically demanding. As the business expanded and she also became interested in making fermented beverages such as mead and the aforementioned kombucha, she had to make choices about where to put her efforts. They discontinued the dairy part of the business and quit offering cheese classes. On a recent trip to the farm, I admired the expanded, meticulously-tended garden and freshly-harvested vegetables, especially the bouquets of varicolored beets, beautiful as any roses, arranged on long tables in the shop and waiting for CSA customers to arrive and collect their weekly shares. I sometimes think I could live on vegetables, but on that visit I did select a fresh chicken from the cooler. It fed us deliciously and well on three subsequent days: roasted, as an ample chicken salad, and, when I had picked it clean and boiled the bones to broth, in a chicken noodle soup.

Shots

It was a beautiful fall day. I walked out to look at the sheep and suddenly gunshots cracked nearby, sending the sheep running up the hill toward the barn. Because the grapes in the surrounding vineyards were getting ripe, at first I wasn't sure whether the sounds were actually guns or just grape cannons. Grape cannons are loud noisemakers set to scare birds away from ripening vineyards and they sound like booming guns. Then I realized the sound wasn't grape cannons.

My first thought was that some idiot was shooting at the sheep. My husband came running around the house. To say he was irritated is a gross understatement. He looked both frightened and ready to strangle somebody. Bullets had whizzed over his head while he was sawing firewood out back. Inside the house we found that the expensive, double-paned sunroom window had been exploded by an almost-spent rifle bullet that now lay between the two panes of broken glass. Bill grabbed the keys to our Ford pickup, and we jumped into the truck, drove out onto our country road, and turned south, the direction the bullets had come from.

As it turned out, the rifle fire was "practice" shots aimed in our direction by a neighbor's adult son, a good old boy of about twenty-nine, and two of his buddies. They didn't believe they were truly causing us any inconvenience or that a bullet could go that far until we insisted they come back to our house and showed them the bullet in the window.

They agreed to pay for the window and apologized in a begrudging way. Later, the most obliging of the three, who works at a local company where we do business, apologized again and told us that we wouldn't have to worry because his buddy's mother "won't let us shoot at his house anymore." I was glad to hear it.

The young men had been shooting toward the woods across from our place, without any concern for what might be on the other side. We and our neighbors live on ten and twenty acre parcels of land. That might sound like a lot of room to someone living on a fifty by one hundred city lot, but the houses aren't that far apart. On a quiet day I can hear a discussion about who misplaced the claw hammer taking place on the deck of the house half a mile down the road, and I can also hear music playing on somebody's barn radio a quarter of a mile in the other direction. The rifle bullet that ended up in our window passed over two ten acre parcels, crossed a busy country road where a school bus and the mailman had just passed, traveled through a small oak woods, penetrated about seven hundred feet into our property, and broke our window.

When we asked the sheriff about regulations governing shooting in the county, he said it's not illegal for people to shoot on their own property so long as they don't endanger others. That last part seemed to be the hitch.

Portland law enforcement had quite the opposite reaction when my nephews and a friend decided to make their own action video, Schwarzenegger style. The kids, between ten and eleven years old, put on camouflage gear and make up and acted out a plot that involved swinging out of their tree house and pretending to kick the daylights out of one another, and then crawling on their bellies across the treacherous landscape of my sister's flower garden. One of their props for this movie was a broken BB gun. The movie, entitled *Terminator Too,* was a hit with their friends.

A couple of weeks later the kids decided to relive the glories of their filmmaking career by running through the yard playing chase with the BB gun. Nick, the oldest, was on the roof of the front porch pretending to shoot at his brother and a friend, when all of a sudden a police car came to a screeching halt in their driveway. Nick had just climbed off the roof when the policeman jumped out of the car, shotgun in hand, and yelled at him to halt and drop his gun. Nick dropped the BB gun as his brother ran in the house calling out to their mom that a policeman was going to shoot Nick.

Without going into all the details I will just say that there followed a tense hour during which the policeman yelled at Nick, yelled at my sister, yelled at anybody else in the neighborhood who would listen, and, as my sister told me later, threatened with the unforgettable words, "I'd blow his head off in a minute. I wouldn't think twice about it. I'd put his brains all over that car, and I wouldn't think twice about it."

Why had this happened? Someone visiting one of their neighbors had seen the kids playing and had called in a report of an armed sniper on the roof.

And why this discrepancy? On the one hand, because of recent dangerous incidents in Portland, the city police must have been too wired to respond with restraint. On the other, the county sheriff's men were either too blasé or too boxed in by the frontier ethic of rural living to crack down on the careless use of guns in the country.

On another day, someone driving down our road saw a deer running across my neighbor's yard and stopped his truck to take a shot, despite the fact that it's illegal to hunt from the road or from a vehicle. He missed the deer but winged the neighbor's deck.

In another incident, a man was picnicking with his family up in the hills not far from here. Someone else was practicing shooting. The picnickers lodged objections. The shooters shot. A man was killed in a dispute over the right to bear arms and fire them.

How far will a shotgun blast travel? A rifle bullet? Farther than people think, apparently.

My father liked guns. He was only mildly interested in hunting, but he liked the craftsmanship, the shape and smell and mechanics of guns. On the Kansas farm where he grew up, guns were taken for granted. I remember one Thanksgiving he won a live turkey at a "turkey shoot," which actually involved shooting at clay pigeons tossed into the air, so I think he was a pretty good shot. He liked making his own gunstocks out of beautiful walnut or cherry wood, but he wasn't terribly attached to any one gun. After he had had a gun for a while, he was like as not to trade it for a different gun or something else—a banjo clock, a camera, a few hours rental on an airplane.

He bought me a BB gun when I was nine or ten. I never wanted to kill anything, though my friends sometimes shot birds. I just liked to shoot at trees, cans, or targets. The gun was pretty. As I remember it had a real wooden stock, not plastic, and on the metal there was an engraved design of a man aiming a gun at a fox. My father also had an air rifle I liked, and he would occasionally let me shoot at telephone poles on the other side of the field, across the street from where we lived in Clatskanie. Without consulting me, one day he traded the air rifle to someone else for something I don't remember, and I had a brief feeling of loss. Then the barrel of the BB gun got bent in packing when we moved to another town, and of course it was never any good after that. I was out of the gun game.

When my first husband and I were impoverished graduate students at the University of Oregon, we had a housemate who used to hunt. I learned to cook venison to go with the government surplus foods we collected at the fairgrounds when times were tough. Every little bit helped in those days.

As an adult, I tried shooting cans at a gravel pit with my dad. It was fun to see what I could hit, but I hated the noise, and my ears rang for days. I wouldn't want to hunt the deer that wander through our place or the gigantic Roosevelt elk that gather in a large, indolent herd up near Hagg Lake in the winter. I might feel like shooting a coyote that goes after our livestock, but when I actually think of doing it, I'm stopped by how beautiful they are and remember that for the most part they eat small rodents. Maybe I could shoot someone breaking into the house, but I hope never to face that situation. I still shudder at the memory of those whizzing rifle bullets that shot out our window.

Recently, a dog came into our field and started chasing the sheep. I followed the dog home in my car and honked in its owner's driveway. The man who came out of the house had a friendly smile and a gigantic decorative buckle on his belt that said, I am not kidding, "Hands Off My Gun."

I told him his dog had been chasing my sheep.

"Hell," he said. "Next time you see him doing that, shoot him. I won't have a dog that chases sheep."

I told him I didn't want to shoot his dog. I just wanted it to stay away from my sheep. He obviously thought I was citified. Maybe I should just get my own belt buckle with a few choice words, as soon as I decide what those words ought to be.

I don't know what it all means, except that the status of guns in our country is an endless conundrum. Tradition, paranoia, feeding a family, revolution, criminality, pride, human ingenuity, war and peace, sport and competition, tragic accidents, old western movies, city versus country—these are just a few of the threads that tangle the issue. If we are going to live with guns, maybe we need to live a lot farther apart. Miles and miles and miles apart.

At Home in the Universe

❖

It's 11:32 p.m. in early November when I turn out the lights and go
to bed. I pull the covers up to my chin and slowly, slowly, so as not
to waken him, I ease my chilly feet up against heat-engine Bill, who
has been asleep since 10:00. I hope I won't just lie here looking at
the clock for an hour or so, but sometimes the world is so intense
it's hard to close my eyes. I look out the big bedroom window to
the east. The sky has cleared, and I realize that another year has
passed, and I am looking at Orion's belt, which has been out of sight
at this hour for the past few months. It is a sweet feeling to see this
beautiful constellation coming round again to tell me it is truly fall.

A decent view of the night sky is one of the advantages of living
in the country.

If I mention to city friends how beautiful Jupiter or Mars have
been lately, they say, oh, is that what that is? They may have noticed
an extra bright light in the sky, but of course the planets lose much
of their magnificence to city illumination, even on moonless nights.
And as for fainter stars and most of the constellations, because of
light pollution they are barely visible in town, if at all.

I got our little telescope for Bill as a Christmas present, and he is
happy to share a peek at Saturn's rings, or Jupiter's moons, or Venus
in a crescent phase, but because he likes to go to bed earlier than
I do, I use it more. Saturn, Venus, Jupiter, and, of course, the amazing surface of the moon, are easy and rewarding sights. I also like to
find the Orion Nebula, which is visible even with our binoculars.
It looks like a spider's cottony egg sac just below Orion's belt. And
sometimes in summer I can see what I believe is M31, the Androm-

eda Galaxy, just to the left of the Northern Cross, though with our little telescope it looks more like a faint ball of smoke in the darkness than the great spiral that appears in astronomy books. Those are the high points of my celestial gazing.

First-time stargazers with amateur telescopes often expect to see the great, whirling shapes of light and color as they appear in books. They end up disappointed because these professional images, captured through large, scientific telescopes, are not only greatly magnified but may have been screened with colored filters or tinted to make them clearer and more dramatic. But I am never disappointed by the celestial objects I find in the sky. If I were never to see anything but Saturn and its rings, I would still find it worthwhile to stay up late and go out in the chilly dark to fiddle with the small lenses and somewhat shaky tripod of the telescope.

I was over sixty before I saw Saturn's rings. I still remember the first time I found this unique planet. I set up the telescope in our front field and tried my best to coordinate the aim of the mechanism with the directions in my night sky guide. Suddenly a glimmer of light seemed to throw a beam across the eyepiece. I moved the telescope in the direction of the beam, and there it was, like a round head wearing a broad-brimmed hat, a still, tiny orb surrounded by its rings. When I brought it into focus the image was very tiny but so remarkable, it seemed to pull me into itself so that its presence filled my eyes, my mind, my whole head. I had only seen it in pictures before, but now I had found it by myself, out in the dark with only the dogs and the owls for company. When I mention Saturn to friends, I am still surprised at how many have never seen the planet and its rings except as an anonymous pinprick of light, or in pictures, and it's exciting to introduce them for the first time. It is hard to explain what a significant and emotional moment that vision can be, but I think many others share my feelings. For me, finding Saturn and its rings feels like a spiritual event, as if the planet were a special treat designed for my viewing, a confirmation of the grand and marvelous nature of the universe. Seeing Jupiter, with its bands and its rotating moons, is similarly remarkable, but I think Saturn is best.

I have not gotten far beyond these easily recognizable objects: Saturn, which sometimes is tipped so that its rings appear as a circling plane and other times appears upright so its rings look more like ears or handles on a jug; Jupiter and four of its moons, the moons always changing places and sometimes disappearing behind their mother planet, as if they were performing a dance; our moon with its startling 3-D surfaces; Venus in its moonlike phases; and the Orion nebula. Mars also often looks lovely. It is recognizable in the telescope as a disk or an orb, rather than simply a pinpoint of light, but it is often as beautiful with the naked eye. It hangs out in the night sky like a piece of candy when it is close and brilliant, as it was this past year, and its warm, reddish color is easy to spot.

Besides these telescopic sights, there are the constellations, celestial visions for the naked eye. Before I got the telescope, like most people I could recognize the Big and Little Dippers, the sisterly cluster of the Pleiades, and the high-flying W of Cassiopeia. I had heard the names of other constellations, but I didn't know them on sight. By spending more time out in the night and checking my star guide as well as online astronomy sites, I have gradually learned more of the constellations and where and when to look for them in their progression through the seasons.

Familiar constellations show us which direction we are going, or facing. Now why that should be satisfying or even slightly important in a world of road signs and GPS technology is hard to explain. I sometimes go to relatively wild places, like the mountains or the eastern Oregon desert, but I have never gotten lost in the woods or needed to guide myself by the stars. And yet I like the feeling of knowing where I am in the dark. Around ten o'clock on a summer night, driving back to Yamhill from Portland, I glance up and notice Sagittarius ahead of me. It appears to float from one side of the valley to the other as the road, going south and west, curves this way and that, and I know I am headed in the right direction.

I also enjoy looking at the constellations during the summer, when we are on the sparsely populated southern Oregon beaches near our cabin in Curry County. They are best seen late at night, as the bonfire is dying down in the sand and darkness takes over. On those beaches the Milky Way spilling across the Northern Cross is especially milky. Back at home in Yamhill, the "teapot," or Sagittarius, is a friendly summer sight as it rises and moves across the sky just above the horizon, not far behind zigzagging Scorpio. Some guides say the Milky Way is the steam coming from the teapot of Sagittarius. The Summer Triangle, with the bright stars of Vega, Deneb, and Altair is another distinct form that shares some of its stars with the Northern Cross and with Cygnus the Swan. It is beautiful not only for its geometric shape but also for the brilliant swath of the Milky Way that crosses it like a river or a ribbon.

It's true that though we live out in the country, somewhat away from city lights, a reddish glow still shows above the Chehalem Mountains, which divide us from Portland and its suburbs. This makes the stars fainter here than in the high desert on the east side of the Cascades or on the dark beach near southern Oregon's Humbug Mountain, where the only visible lights are a few distant lanterns on fishing boats offshore.

This past summer, Bill and I splurged on a trip to Italy to meet up with relatives who were staying in Lucca. That area was the home of Puccini and hosts a summer Puccini festival. We had all purchased tickets for Puccini's opera, Tosca, to be performed at night at the Torre del Lago outdoor amphitheater by the lake. During intermission I glanced up at the starlit sky and suddenly realized I was again looking at the stars of the summer triangle, essentially as I would have seen them from my own front yard at this time of year. Universally speaking, we had not traveled so far.

After years of living in the country I have adapted to darkness. It no longer has a mournful feeling, and I love the excuse to go out with the dogs at night and stare into space. The owls call and sometimes there are other bird noises in the dark, or the mooing of a cow on the other side of the valley. There are interludes of howling coyotes, sometimes far off, sometimes crossing our own fields. Occasionally a skunk wanders across the landscape, and if I am lucky I notice it before the dogs do, so I can quickly usher them indoors. Maggie stays clear of skunks, but Guy never seems to stay clear enough.

We do have an electric yard light, but it can be switched off. I think it would be sad to live in a world continually lit by artificial light, with never a clear view of the stars. There is something about the country dark that feels safe and comfortable, like a cape of invisibility. If it's chilly out, I bundle up in the brown wool blanket that Bill spun and wove years ago from the fleece of a black sheep, and I melt into the darkness. It's good to feel at home in the universe.

Cats That Stray and Cats That Stay

❖

We often see stray cats passing through. People with unwanted cats or kittens sometimes drop them in the country, imagining the cats will find a home at a nearby farm. In reality most of them suffer hungry, short lives. I know that large, feral cat colonies sometimes develop, maybe because people feed them or maybe because they represent a burgeoning population of related cats holding their own, but for the most part wandering cats on our farm appear singly. They spend a little time hunting in our fields or show up in the driveway at night and then disappear fearfully into the dark when I call them. These wild cats sometimes remind me of the cats we saw at the Protestant cemetery in Rome, where the poet Keats is buried. There the cats gather for people who feed them in the sunken area near the first-century BC Roman pyramid on the edge of the cemetery. The pyramid makes an exotic spot for a feral cat colony, and there is a donation box in the cemetery for cat food.

I also remember the cats that populated the roofs in Corfu, Greece, when I lived there fifty years ago. Women would reach out of upper story windows and put food for them on the rooftops. Perhaps the cats were various colors, but in my memory they were mainly black and white, an inbred population that was fed and tolerated both out of humanitarian impulse and as a way of keeping rodents in check. Cats have a long history of interdependence with human society, but at the same time they maintain a certain aloofness and more easily survive on their own than dogs.

For many years on the farm we had several cats of our own. When we first moved here, I put out a call for kittens. A friend gave us two tabbies, Colette and Gigi, who happily lived with us into their old age. About the same time, my daughter in Seattle caught two wild kittens from a litter she'd found in a garage and brought them to us. Later, when another daughter was attending graduate school at the University of Arizona, she found a stray, short-haired, gray cat, which is how we acquired young Valencia (named for Valencia Street in Tucson). A third daughter, who was going to school in San Diego, found a large, gray, elderly cat she couldn't keep, named her Finders, and sent her to us by air. We had all the cats spayed, and they got their regular shots and meds. That was more than enough cats for many years.

When the first four kittens were growing up we kept them in the house, but after they were adults we eventually let them out and they became barn cats, sleeping in the straw bales we used for sheep bedding. The barn was airy, comfortable, and warmed at night by the presence of the sheep. To make it even more comfortable I arranged old blankets and towels as cat beds in the straw. The cats tolerated one another but staked out separate sleeping spots.

I've read that domestic cats may claim four or five acres as their territory, while feral cats roam around three hundred or more, but so far as I could tell most of our cats didn't go far at all. When we went outside they frequently meandered up to greet us. Colette, GiGi, and Valencia especially liked our company and would follow us with the dogs when we took walks around the farm. These three also took on the role of territorial defenders and would chase other wandering cats off the place.

The two feral kittens from Seattle, Simone and Brownie, however, were a different matter. They were beautiful cats, and we tried to socialize them but it never really worked. Brownie was a warm-brown tabby. Simone was a tiny cat with the coloring of a Siamese: a dark brown mask on her champagne-colored face, brown paws and ear tips, and a naturally bobbed tail. She was especially adorable looking. Of course, I wanted all the kittens to like us and be happy. We handled them and kept them in the house until they were grown, but these two Seattle cats remained perpetually wild. Even indoors they would hide much of the time, rarely coming out except to eat. The only time they seemed to like human company was when Bill stretched out in his big leather chair with his feet on the footstool, watching TV. Then they would sometimes climb onto his stomach purring and kneading his shirt. But if he reached for them and showed any sign of being a person instead of a warm cushion, they would take off. Wild animals from the start, these two were spooked by noises of the furnace or our movements around the house. When they submitted to being petted their bodies were rigid and ready to run. They almost seemed to stop breathing when we picked them up. As they got older, they became more and more intolerant of the other cats and showed tension and fear if the dogs even looked at them. To escape seemed their main desire.

I finally gave up on ever taming the two wild ones and tried to adapt them to the barn. Even with their freedom, neither would stay near the other cats. They would come around to be fed but were extremely nervous about it. Simone chose to sleep alone on the high tractor seat in the machine shed, and I fed her there. Even when I set food out and backed away, Brownie would watch from a distance before eating. Eventually she took to climbing onto the roof of the house around feeding time, so I would stand precariously on a bench and stretch to place her food dish at the edge of the roof where she apparently felt safe enough to eat. The scenario reminded me of the Greek women feeding cats on the rooftops of Corfu.

These two wild cats became more and more remote over the years and eventually disappeared. I imagine they suffered the fate of most wild cats and met some accident or predator. In a happier scenario, perhaps they found a household with no other cats or dogs, and were adopted and tamed as I could never tame them. The remaining cats lived long and apparently happy lives on the farm.

After many years, our aging cat population was declining when another cat appeared. One morning I found a beautiful, long-haired, black and orange female cat mewing on the side deck. She was large, like a Maine Coon cat, but looked as if she had been starved. I got her a bowl of cat food and happily imagined taking her in as our new cat. When I put the food dish on the deck, however, she didn't start eating. Instead she paced back and forth mewing loudly. What a surprise—from the underside of the deck up popped two orange kittens. She made purring and meowing sounds, and the two kittens raced to the dish and began to eat. She didn't eat till they had finished. What a good mother.

I had no idea where this starved beauty and the kittens had come from, unless someone had dropped them off. Since we had three other cats at this time, I thought I would keep the mother, have her spayed, and look for homes for the two kittens. I already knew one friend who was looking for a cat, her old cat having died a few months earlier. After I fed them, I put out a blanket in a box on the deck, hoping to make them feel at home, but the mother cat and kittens retired under the deck and out of reach. The next morning I came out to find that the mother had disappeared with one of the kittens and left the other, who came running when I rattled a food dish. I can only think she must have been on a trip to distribute her kittens. Would a cat behave in this way? Wild female cats may drive their male offspring away, though in this case she seemed to be passing them around in a caring manner instead. I wondered if there had been others dropped off before she came to our house. Bill christened the orange kitten Ockley. We took him to the vet for neutering and shots, and he moved into the house.

Ockley was a charming kitten. He would stand on his hind legs and insolently box the older cats with his front paws, then take off running, his soft feet making unbelievably loud galloping noises on the floor. The old lady cats put up with it, not giving him so much as a hiss. He was good with the dogs, cuddly with us, and showed no fear of anything or anybody. In the fall, when we had walnuts drying in pans near the woodstove, he would pluck one out with his teeth or a paw and spend hours knocking the walnut loudly around the house. His one fault was that he was an extremely skilled hunter of birds. He would crouch in the grass and then make impossibly high leaps in the air to catch a bird flying by. Even hummingbirds were not safe from his wild leaps, so we kept him in the house most of the time.

We hoped and expected to have the delightful company of Ockley for many years. When we let him out for brief periods, he would often play one of his games, which was to run up and down the branches of the oak tree on the south side of the house. It was a huge, old tree, its long branches reaching like arms away from the house and far beyond its base. It was hard to believe, since he seemed so quick and agile, but I think Ockley must have fallen from that tree. One day we found him lying dead beneath the branches he loved to climb. Contrary to popular belief, cats can fall, and they don't always land on their feet. There was no other explanation. Years later I still feel sadness at losing delightful Ockley. For a long time we found walnuts in odd corners and under furniture where he had left them in one of his walnut-soccer games.

One by one, our other cats lived out long lives and went to cat heaven, until finally we had no cats at all. A couple of years passed, when one day we began to see a large, orange tom hanging around. He kept his distance, but when I tried rattling cat food in a pan and calling kitty-kitty he seemed interested. I would put the food out and then back off, and he began to come and eat. Finally he came up without my backing away. I reached out to pet him and was surprised when he rubbed his head against my hand and rolled over, inviting more attention. He was thin and ragged, and he flattened his ears when our dogs came out of the house and tried to stare him down, but he didn't run, so they didn't chase. Eventually I was able to pick him up and put him in the little building behind the house, where I gave him a cat bed and food and water. A few days after he moved in, I was petting him when I found a large cyst on his neck, an infection of the sort that might have come from a catfight. Bill the cat namer had started calling him Pinky. Giving a stray cat a name is the first step toward a relationship.

I called the vet and took Pinky in to treat the cyst, which had grown hot and big as a golf ball, and also with the intention of having him neutered and given shots. The vet looked him over and said, "We can give him his shots but I don't think he needs to be neutered." Besides the obvious, which hadn't been obvious to me, she pointed to one of his ears. The tip had been clipped off. "Some cat rescue people don't even try to rescue all the cats in a wild cat colony," the vet told me, "but they do trap and neuter them, and then release them back into the wild. Removing a population of wild breeding cats is only temporary. If there is a cat vacuum, other feral cats will soon move in. If they are neutered and released that keeps the population down and keeps other cats out. The clipped ear is a sign that this was done."

That still left shots and the infection to be tended to. The vet and an assistant began the nasty but necessary job of draining the infection on his neck. I covered my nose with my scarf as a horrible smell filled the room. After the cyst had been drained of the thick yellow pus, they cleaned the wound and provided antibiotic tablets for the infection, an antibiotic topical salve, and a solution for washing his wound. Pinky took it surprisingly well and behaved with docility through the whole ordeal.

The vet estimated he was at least five years old, not a young cat. That was over three years ago, so he may be eight now or older. He has adapted beautifully. He is affectionate and friendly. Our incorrigible dogs would love to herd him, but when they give him the border collie eye and dare him to run, he just stands his ground. Sometimes he tries to win them over by rubbing affectionately against them. They obviously consider this freakish and embarrassing cat behavior and back off. Sometimes I wonder if he was truly ever a wild cat. Perhaps he was someone's pet that got trapped one night when he was out tangling with the wild ones. He certainly seems domesticated. And yet, though he has adapted completely to us, when other people come to the house he hides, a last sign of his wild life. If I mention our cat, visitors say they are surprised to hear that we even have one, since they never see him.

Pinky has a large, pleasant face. He reminds me of Sam, the orange tomcat my son had about forty years ago. His eyes are gold, with black slits to let the light in. His white whiskers curve gently downward on each side, and the variegated dark and light orange stripes in his tabby fur suggest life in a jungle or forest, where bright sun might burn through cooling leaves in striped patterns.

He has gained weight in the years since he arrived, and his fur is thick and sleek. I like to hold him and he likes to be held. Once in a while he comes into the house, but he never settles down. He walks around briefly, looks things over, then grows uneasy, and goes to the door where he gives a drawn-out, mournful sort of meow, obviously wanting out. When it is getting dark he still goes into the little building out back to eat and curl up in his bed. We close the door of the building at night, but even in the daytime when we leave the door ajar he is often curled sleeping in his bed or sitting quietly on the porch of "his" house, watching the world go by.

It's good to have a cat again.

Grace

Where do our preferences in life come from? What events, what choices, made even before we were born, helped shape the lives we lead? And how will our lives now affect those of our children and grandchildren and beyond? It's good to remember that we live in a continuum whether we think much about it or not.

My mother recently gave me copies of a post card and two letters sent in 1939 and 1941 from my Kansas grandmother, Grace Wardrope Robertson, to her half-brother Jimmie in Oklahoma. The originals were copied years ago by my brother when he was investigating family genealogy and visited a descendant of Jimmie's. The messages foreshadow where my own life would turn.

I was tremendously moved when I read the letters over seventy years later. Grace lived through the Dustbowl and the Great Depression, lost her mother when she was only four, saw the family farm seized by a bank fattening on Depression foreclosures, endured the early death of her husband, and faced the uncertain years of World War II. My grandmother's life was harder than mine, and yet she sounds like a happy person who loved living and kept a good outlook. After they lost their farm to the bank, she and my grandfather rented another place and continued to raise sheep on leased fields.

Both Grace and my paternal grandfather James were nearby when I was born on April 13, 1939, in Abilene, Kansas. Grandmother Grace visited my mother in the hospital every day during the long lying-in that was common back then. She brought apple blossoms, which my mother assures me were in full bloom in Kansas on my birthday. I like to think my grandmother blessed me with her optimistic nature along with those blossoms.

Shortly after that, when I was five months old and we were still living in Kansas, Grace's husband, my grandfather James, died suddenly after four days of fever and in the midst of a busy life, leaving my grandmother and their two sons, my father, Ward, and his younger brother, Stewart, to carry on as best they could. The brevity of Grace's post card to her brother Jimmie, announcing her husband's death, startled me at first. Nowadays a death in the family brings a flurry of phone calls, e-mails, a car trip or the purchase of plane tickets. In depression era 1939, the distance between Abilene, Kansas, and Edith, Oklahoma, must have seemed long. The farmhouse did not yet have electricity in 1939, but my mother tells me there was a phone. Maybe calling long distance was too expensive or difficult. Post cards were the e-mail of those days. In any case, my grandmother sent news of my grandfather's death in this brief, understated communication.

Postcard from Grace Robertson to James L. Wardrope Edith, Oklahoma, postmarked Abilene, Kansas, September 30, 1939

Jimmie,
    Jim died last nite at the hospital here. He was only ill a few days and bad only a few hours. Four doctors could not save him and could not diagnosis it. Will write you.
    Grace R.

Her next, longer letter to Jimmie tells more in detail about my grandfather's passing and the final diagnosis of his illness, and also explains new arrangements for my father and his brother, Stewart, to take over the family sheep business. She alludes to dry Dustbowl weather and mentions how much she wants to visit the family in Oklahoma. Her own father, my father's grandfather, was still alive at the time, and she hoped for a future visit.

Letter from Grace Robertson, 1939

Dear Folks,

I wanted to write you but kept thinking that maybe we might find a way to come and planned to several times but Ward and his wife and baby (Barbara Ann) [my father, mother, and I] rented this place and moved here with Stewart and me. And Stewart took over Jim's sheep business since you were here. So with feeding lambs and lambing ewes here at home, and Stewart getting sheep in as you remember at the yards and selling, you can readily see how hard it is to get away but we are watching for a lull and will come but I am afraid now it will have to be in the spring. Because the boys just got a load of feeding lambs today and won't be rid of them before 6 or 8 weeks.

Jim was only ill not alarmingly from Sun till Thur [when] he became delirious and we took him to the hospital Thur eve thinking he might have typhoid but 4 doctors could not find what ailed him or do anything for him and he passed away Fri eve. Monday we received the report from Topeka that they found the virus of Encephalitis or sleeping sickness similar to the horse disease. They know nothing about it, how people get it or how to treat it but 99 out of a 100 cases have proved fatal or leave the patient paralyzed or worse (insane). We can't seem to get used to not looking for him in the evening. He had been so busy with the sheep this year, had sold 6 or 8 loads that month but was happy with the work. We are so glad that the boys are so busy now and can carry on and I try to help a little (mostly choreing, picking cobs etc).

It has been dry here too not so much as a little west of here but we do not have wheat pasture as in other years, and it has been so warm here all fall. Write me and we will come

the first time it is possible. Ward wants to so much and wants to come while dad is still well and about. I would like to see the youngsters too. Ward is taking a bunch of pictures to send you of their wonderful granddaughter and the family.
Grace

Grace's letter provides a revealing look at life before antibiotics. In the words about encephalitis, I sense my grandmother seizing, in her grief, on a doctor's assurance that her husband's passing was better than living with the long-term effects of the disease. Several pictures of my grandfather show him on horseback, always with a lasso and a gun and wearing a cowboy hat. He studied agriculture at Kansas State College and introduced a new variety of sheep into Kansas; his first sale of 740 of these breeding ewes was covered by *Life* magazine, and the future looked promising. He was full of energy and promise. Then he died at the age of fifty-two. In 1939, in the last years of the Depression, there would have been little for my grandmother to fall back on.

There is nevertheless a happy note at the end of the letter. My father was a photographer, and my memories of him will always involve the smell of developer, stop bath, and hypo in a quiet darkroom. I am pleased to know he was already practicing his lifelong passion for photography and cameras when I was born.

Grace's third letter, written two years later, reveals the family in very different places.

Kansas City Mo. Dec. 10, 41
Dear Brother Jimmie and family:
    As the holidays roll around we think more of our friends and relatives. You probably would be surprised where we all are. Ward, his wife and Baby are living near Portland, Oregon. Stewart, his wife and little red head blue-eyed baby [my cousin Annie] live in an apartment in Abilene but he is in the

Civil Service (a Junior Checker) at Funston near Fort Riley, has been there for nearly a year—And I'm here nursing. I've been here since the 28 of April. And probably will be for a few months yet. After Ward and Monie [my mother Monica's nickname] moved in with me when Dad died and Stewart got married I decided I would try practical nursing and was never home long enough to get rested. This is a very pleasant case, a chest case (TB) and a little 3 ½ year girl who was born with club feet and has been in and out of casts her entire life. But our home is new in a new restricted district and small, only 5 or 6 rooms and very comfortable and efficient. We had a sale the last day of March and moved from the river farm which was very fortunate for us. As it completely flooded 4 times and yet is so wet as to make it impossible to get to. I get very lonesome for my family and home but it is not so bad when I am busy. We go to the hospitals very frequently and I shop for the house once a week and am just one of the family here so it is not so bad. I am planning to go to Abilene for a few days, Christmas week. I still call Aunt Mary's and Uncle Jake's Home. What did the summer do to you? It rained so much I imagine you had good crops and lots of grass and feed. Is Basil in the draft age, of course both Ward & Stewart are. Things do not sound too good around the world. Lucerne's Bob [Grace's nephew] is on the Pacific somewhere. Her next son was working here in Kans. City last summer. I've not seen Lucerne since I saw you folks but we go down near there to the hospital (T.B.) at Mt Vernon Mo. and I may yet be able to go to see her and her family before I leave here.

Do you ever see any sheep? I get homesick every time I see one. They have been a good piece of property the past few years. Write me sometime soon and tell me how Dad is and wish him a Pleasant Christmas and a comfortable New Year for me. I would like some pictures of all of you. So I

will close wishing all of you a Joyous Christmas and a Happy
New Year. And Marie, an extra wish for you.
Your sister Grace Robertson
8117 Meadow Lane
Kansas City, Mo.

P. S. You can always get in touch with me thru Uncle Jake's
in care of. Mrs. J. B. Hostetter, 306 E 7th, Abilene, Kans. [Af-
ter the death of her mother my grandmother was raised by
her mother's sister, Aunt Mary Hostetter, and Mary's husband, Uncle Jake.]

For such a short, personal letter there is a lot of implied history. The years of the Dust Bowl had ended and instead there were
heavy rains and floods. Kansas City was apparently segregated, with
"restricted" neighborhoods. I asked my mother about my grandmother's working situation, and she told me the woman with tuberculosis had been treated and her disease was considered inactive at
the time. Tuberculosis still exists worldwide but nowadays it is rare
in the United States. I wondered if the child's clubfoot was related
to her mother's illness. Today, at least in the United States, treatment
for clubfoot is so universal, we rarely see an untreated case. And then
there was the reference to the young male relatives eligible for the
draft, a dire hint of events to come. After the depression years, who
could count on anything? There must have been enormous uncer-
tainty about the future.

And yet my young parents were optimistic and adventurous. In
1941 they sold their sheep, the modest return for which was their
stake in a new place. They bought a new pickup, filled the back with
their few belongings, and moved west, leaving Kansas the day after
I turned two. We took Route 66 to California. My memory kicks
in when we arrived in Los Angeles, and I got my first neck-bending
look at palm trees, a lofty image forever stamped in my mind. From
there we drove north to Oregon.

I know now that Kansas is beautiful in its own way, but I can also imagine how the difference between Oregon and Kansas must have been heightened by the midwestern droughts of the 1930s. Mom remembers people hanging wet blankets over windows during dust storms and how they worried about asphyxiation or pneumonia from the flying dust. When she was sixteen and dating my twenty-one year old father, she tells me, he came to pick her up one day and she immediately noticed he was radiating heat. His temperature proved to be 104. After several days of getting up at 3 a.m. to spray swarms of grasshoppers on the parched fields of the farm before the insects began feeding for the day, my father had come down with dust pneumonia. He survived, obviously, but he spent many days in bed, being nursed back to health by his mother Grace.

When my father proposed he promised my mother that if she married him he would take her to Oregon, which he had visited once. Compared to the green, mountainous Northwest, Kansas in the Great Depression years must have looked flat, desolate, and dry.

After the move, my young mother was naturally lonesome for her large family, and so, in the autumn of 1942, a year and a half after we had moved away, my mother and I took a Greyhound bus from Oregon back to Kansas. In 1942, buses were always full. War-time gas rationing made bus travel a popular and necessary form of transportation. I was a curious three year old on a long trip in the company of strangers, and so I stared at faces and listened to conversations all across the country. I remember a little boy traveling alone. He must have been eight or nine, and I was impressed that he wore a boy-size fedora and a wool coat over his pants and shirt—to me he looked like a miniature adult man. I don't know how far he traveled, but he had his travel information pinned to his coat and everyone on the bus seemed to be taking care of him. I also remember two pretty, young women sitting together. They passed the time laughing and chatting brightly or singing in harmony. The song I remember them singing was "When It's Springtime in the Rockies." Perhaps we were crossing those defining mountains at the time, and the words, "I'll be coming back to you," were appropriate for the journey.

Of course, buses didn't have restrooms in those days, and there were no public rest areas along the two-lane roads, but when I insisted I had to go potty the driver obligingly stopped in the middle of the great plains without a restroom anywhere in sight so my mom could take me off to the roadside to relieve myself and thus not wet my panties. I don't remember this part of the trip at all, so it was apparently not that exciting to me, but I've heard the story of the obliging bus driver more than once.

Back in Kansas we stayed at mom's comfortable family home in Chapman. The Lorsons owned and ran a large hardware store and John Deere business as well as a Chevrolet dealership. Life there had always been secure and comfortable. My maternal Grandmother Mary invited Grandmother Grace to come and stay while we were there. It was the last time I saw her.

Mom tells me it was during that visit she realized where she really belonged. When we eventually returned to Oregon, again by Greyhound, she was happy to come back to my dad and to the forests and green valleys of western Oregon. It was then that she knew that following him out west had been the right thing to do.

Not long after that visit, in 1942, Grace died of cancer at what now seems the very young age of fifty-one. Although I was just three the last time I saw her, I remember her well. It seems I even remember the sound of her voice. Reading her letters now, I am moved by my grandmother's sweet and enduring character in the face of hardship.

When Grandmother Grace wrote to her brother Jimmie, "Do you ever see any sheep? I get homesick every time I see one," I know a little of how she felt. Now that we no longer have lambs and our flock of sheep has dwindled to one old lady, Pinknose, I sometimes find myself staring at someone else's pretty sheep with nostalgia, especially when they resemble our multi-colored Romneys. At least a couple of local farms still have descendants of our sheep. I imagine offering the farmers a good price for a starter flock, four or five lambs maybe, from which I might begin all over. I could even give them names starting with A, as we did with our first-year lambs, Amity, Aurora, and Ajax, and it would be a new beginning. Then I shake myself awake. I'm too old to wrestle a 150-plus pound sheep into getting its feet trimmed or to stay up all night waiting for lambs; really, there's no going back.

I think of my grandmother now because I am reading her letters, but also because of the stories I heard all my life about when the family raised sheep on the Kansas farm. I loved listening to the one about the bummer lamb she bottle raised in the fenced-in farmhouse yard. It grew to be a head-butting ram, which, according to my dad, threatened everyone but her. I loved hearing about the days before my memory, when I lived on the farm, struggling to pronounce the word alfalfa and keeping company with a border collie named Fannie that worked the sheep. I am thankful in many ways to that grandmother who died over seventy years ago, and who left me an inclination to sheep and border collies, a love of country life, and an optimistic outlook. She is surely one of the reasons I live as I do today.

Everybody Talks About the Weather

❖

Once more it's the autumnal equinox. Time passes like sun-sparkles dancing on a lake. We take our usual daily dog walk: past the neighboring young vineyard; past the old English walnut trees being overtaken by their black walnut rootstock; past the white hive boxes set out in Farmer Dromgoole's alfalfa field where the bees idle around as if wondering, where have all the flowers gone?

There's no traffic on the road, but I keep Maggie on a leash because she is recovering from an unknown poisoning that almost killed her last week. I don't want to take a chance of her lapping water from a roadside ditch that might be contaminated with some unhealthy runoff. The neighboring vineyard is advertised as organic, but I still worry. Perhaps she ate something bad when we visited the beach last week. The vet can only guess the cause and treat the illness. Now I'm just happy to see that the yellow of jaundice has gone from her eyes. The whites are back to a healthy blue-white, and she seems full of energy.

In spite of such worries, the day is beautiful. A light rain scrubbed the air to clean brightness. In the west, the Coast Range is a deep blue I can imagine sketching with pastels on fine-toothed gray paper. The distant hills are a study in graduated values, all the way down the valley.

When my niece Marie's in-laws came to Oregon for her wedding to Klaus, his Italian aunts remarked that our wine country landscape reminded them of Tuscany. I've been to Tuscany and believe that the hill towns, towers, and churches grace the landscape in a way that can't be duplicated anywhere else, but I was pleased that they found a Tuscan beauty in our vineyards and rolling hills. It is gratifying to see ourselves as inhabitants of a special place.

It has been a rainy summer. The heat started late and ended early, and, with such a short season, at the end of September the grapes are still not ripe. The neighboring vineyard we walk past is three years old, and this year would be their first harvest. Today we see that workers have been taking off clusters of grapes and tearing off the sheltering lower leaves to expose remaining bunches. This should help to ripen them before the fall rain sets in and wrecks the fruit. A stretch of sunny weather has been predicted, and we also have hopes for our own grapes, many of which Bill has similarly exposed by removing foliage. The pinot noir clusters have turned purple but the brix, or sugar content, is still too low. Some of the chardonnays are developing that translucent golden look that means they are ripening, but many are still green.

The word from the commercial vineyards, announced in the newspapers, is that it will be a late harvest, possibly scant, but the wine may be extraordinary. Whatever the conditions, the winemakers always say the wine may be extraordinary, may being the important qualifier, and it could well be true. Wine is complicated, and even hardship sometimes does amazing things. Our own pinot noir, largely organic, made with amateur and small-time equipment, is different every year. Some years it is so delicious we feel rich and privileged. In such years it makes meals seem like a sacrament. Other years it is just wine.

We do feel privileged here. We aren't rich and our margin of economic security is narrow, but so far we are more than fine. Our greater wealth lies in the beauty of the place: the contours of the land, wildflowers, good, local food, the nearness of coast, mountains, and high desert, the bounty of family and friends. In books, in art, in creative pursuits.

I hope for as good a life for our children and grandchildren. And yet every day brings news of a world at risk, including an alarming slide into climate change and its consequences.

Last week local television featured a story on what to expect of the wine industry, in view of climate change. One of the predictions was that due to warming, more California grape growers and winemakers will be looking north and buying up valuable vineyard property in our area. This is already happening. The International Pinot Noir Celebration, held annually at my college, brings wine aficionados and business people from all over the world. Some vintners from abroad have also bought and planted Yamhill County land. At the local level, the Yamhill Carlton High School has begun a program to teach students how to manage vineyards and prepare them for future jobs in the industry. With the backing of area vintners the students have planted rows of wine grapes right next to the high school baseball field.

There is a tinge of satisfaction in these stories about our area becoming the next Napa-Sonoma or the American Burgundy. But that's looking on the bright side, following a year in which the contiguous United States had the hottest year on record and the Northwest had one of its wettest years. If the climate continues to heat up, there may be far more problems than advantages for the world at large. Desertification, water shortages, forest fires, famines, displaced world populations—you name it.

This past year, forest fires burned thousands of acres in the dry southern Oregon Siskiyou Mountains and on the east side of the Cascades. Is there anything we can do? In a recent *New York Times* article, one writer says that we have the means to deal with climate change but wonders if we have the will to do it. He refers to the collective will of societies, governments, and the world at large. And what about individuals?

Some people don't believe in climate change, don't want to think about it, or feel that it's someone else's problem. Most of us feel small in the big picture. If we recycle newspapers and send our vegetable scraps and coffee grounds into the garden instead of a landfill, there's satisfaction about doing the right thing, but then we see news pictures of Styrofoam and plastic wrap rolling across ocean bottoms or read a story about bees dying from agricultural spray in a nearby town. It's discouraging. Are we at a tipping point or is it too late? And when our lives are relatively comfortable, or conversely if economic problems threaten local families, how can we be moved to deal with problems in other parts of the world? Given the odds, it's sometimes hard to act, especially when life is good. But whatever we do or don't do in our time will have long-term results for our children and grandchildren, just as economic, agricultural, and international policy affected the lives and times of my grandparents and parents. For me, it always comes back to the children.

When we talk about climate change, we need to distinguish between weather and climate. Weather means day-to-day temperature, wind, moisture, and general atmospheric conditions. It is pretty much beyond our control. So far as weather goes, all we can do is cope. Insulate. Buy a fan. Put on a warm sweater. But climate is the overall pattern of weather over time, and it is much more difficult to see, predict, influence, and understand, especially since we humans tend to focus on the day-to-day. Climate is now, but it also includes what hasn't happened yet. Maybe it's not yet too late to influence the future.

I remember many examples of extreme weather from my own lifetime. As a child living along the Columbia River in 1948, I saw the devastating Vanport Flood, which wiped out a city. Vanport City was a government housing project just outside of Portland, built for around forty thousand people working in wartime shipyards. Shortly after the flood, my parents drove from Washington into Portland, and I saw masses of crushed, muddy debris. In that devastated landscape, the most pathetic detail to me, as a child, was a lone toilet, still attached to a piece of wrecked flooring, floating downstream.

I was in grade school during the record-breaking Northwest winters of 1948 and 1950, when the surface of deep snow was topped with a crackling layer of ice that threatened my shins like a knife blade. Telephones and electricity were out for days. My father, the local telephone man, worked nonstop during both of those stormy winters, repairing fallen telephone lines. One night he came back to our candle-lit home to snatch a quick nap. I heard him whispering to my mother that he'd found a frozen body near the train tracks where he was repairing telephone lines that had snapped under the weight of ice.

And there was the famous Columbus Day storm of 1962, which I missed because I was living in Greece at the time. Europe also had its extreme weather during the winter of 1962 to 1963. Newspapers announced that it was the coldest winter since Napoleon invaded Russia. Water on the Riviera froze. In spite of being out of the country that Columbus Day, I saw plenty of evidence of the storm when my husband and I returned to Oregon the following year. We rented a tiny cabin in the woods outside Portland. Much of the forest was still standing, but on the ground were hundreds of fallen trees the previous year's Columbus Day storm had dropped like matchsticks.

I remember the great flood of 1964, when roads between the Willamette Valley and the coast were cut off and houses floated like toy ducks down the Umpqua River to the sea. I remember a record breaking January freeze in 1980, the same year Mount St. Helens erupted several times, the volcano alternately coating cars and landscape with light volcanic ash or a soupy gray rain, depending on the wind and weather.

Sometimes extreme or unusual weather seems fortunate. When we moved to this Yamhill farm, I complained that our living room was too dark, and Bill bravely took a saw to the end of the house in order to add a light-gathering sunroom. Conveniently for us—and who doesn't measure weather to a certain extent by their own comfort?— it didn't rain till almost Christmas, by which time Bill had finished the job. Such autumn dryness is extremely rare in western Oregon, but nature favored us that year, and the sunroom is still a welcome light well in any season.

I could continue to drag up extremes from memory: the year we were snowed in for Christmas; the year the Yamhill Valley flooded, and the Tualatin River and all its little tributaries came over the roads; the year a freakish southwest wind howled up from the coast and blew down our old barn. We have seen years with so much spring rain the bees couldn't pollinate the fruit trees and fruit was scant, and years when trees were so well pollinated heavy crops of apples broke branches to the ground.

And yet all of these fluctuations are weather, anomalous events in a general climate pattern. When we get a disastrous storm or a blistering week of sunshine, we hope and believe that if we just wait, things will get back to normal. We have car chains, flashlights, a small Coleman stove, canned food, bottled water. On hot days our house stays fairly cool without air conditioning, and when it gets too hot we have electric fans and ice to cool our drinking water. We live in a temperate climate. Normally our weather is very comfortable. But what if normal changes, as is predicted? How much change can people tolerate? What will the future bring to Yamhill County? To the Willamette Valley? To Oregon and beyond? What about the water table and our precious wells? What about the wildflowers and lungworts? I think back seventy years, a lifetime and yet not so long really. Now I think seventy years into the future. I won't be around, but will our beloved grandchildren inherit a world of damage? I fervently hope not.

Fluctuations in climate have always been influenced by natural causes such as variations in solar energy or volcanic eruptions, but nowadays, human activity, in the form of increased population and carbon emission, has been firmly linked to climate change. And our immediate world has changed. When Bill and I bought this place and were in the slow process of moving out here, via a borrowed pickup and our car, I noticed that west of the Portland city limits we came to a stretch of new roads. Nothing was built along these roads, but they were wide, nicely paved, and lined with what looked like city streetlights. Naively I wondered why anyone would go to such expense to build roads and infrastructure so far out in the country.

It was several years before anything much happened on these roads, and then it seemed almost overnight houses and condominiums appeared along with shopping malls, fast food restaurants, and high tech businesses. If we drove south from Portland and then west, the other route from Portland to Yamhill, the same thing happened. Little, empty country roads my carpool once used to make a quick exit from the city have become urban shopping areas and housing subdivisions. An evergreen forest I used to admire along the Tualatin-Sherwood road was logged and the land, instead of being replanted with trees, was turned into an enormous junkyard for wrecked cars. Nearby McMinnville, where I taught college before retiring and where we do most of our shopping, grew from 13,000 when we moved here to over 32,000 today.

Our thought that we would one day move back to the city now seems almost beside the point. In many ways the city has come to us.

There are still lots of farms growing wheat, grass seed, berries, hazelnuts, grapes, and nursery plants, but the exits from the Sunset Highway, a busy route connecting Portland to the beach, have undergone major road work, the addition of two-lane ramps, lights to control the flow of traffic, and massive overpasses.

Sometimes environmentalists speak of "smart growth." An example would be ultra-dense housing where people could live, work, and shop, all within walking distance, and where economical public transportation would be conveniently available. Such density would leave large natural spaces outside the populated areas. I remember a newspaper feature in the comic pages of Sunday newspapers when I was growing up. Each week geophysicist and oceanographer Athelston Spilhaus would publish a colored comic strip putting forth some information on science. I still recall his proposal for a linear city, where high-density housing mixed with nearby places for work and shopping and a central transportation system would wind across the landscape like a snake. At the boundaries of the "snake" there would be vast natural areas untouched by human development. It was my first encounter with the concept of "smart growth," the idea of controlling development in order to preserve rural and natural land. I have to say the commercial, interior aspects of the snake-shaped development interested me far less than the prospect of everyone having a natural landscape on the other side of their building.

How might our twenty acres compare to what might constitute a high-density, "smart growth" model for living? I looked for examples of density and found far-ranging estimates. Our densest population in the United States is in New York City, with approximately forty-three people per acre. If we had that same density our little farm would have about 860 people living on it. Nearby Portland supports about 6.6 persons per acre, though some neighborhoods are much denser than that. For us that would mean 132 people living in our yard, walking their dogs, putting out their garbage cans, parking their cars. It sounds unbearable now that I have grown accustomed to space.

I started on this train of thought when I wondered whether we should, or ever would, move from this place back to the city. I know that if you like it, living on acreage in the country, even in a small, old farmhouse, is a wonderful luxury. Though I have also lived in cities and enjoyed the ease of connection, I have gotten too used to all this beautiful space and privacy to make the move, unless I were pressed by health, financial, or other reasons. Some day that might happen, but I hope not soon.

Bill and I have a routine of walking every morning. As this morning's walk winds down and we approach the corner of Lilac Hill and Goodrich, we hear a racket that turns out to be the power company with a dozen workers and several monstrous trucks upgrading the electric poles and lines. They have been coming and going along this road all week, careful to make sure our electrical interruptions are brief and not too inconvenient. The infrastructure is holding.

The men working on the lines remind me of the many changes technology has brought in the twenty-five years we have lived here. When we moved to Yamhill County in 1987, not really so long ago in old-lady terms, the only local phone calls we could make were to nearby Yamhill and environs and to Grand Island, a farming community about twenty miles away. Everything else was long distance. Nowadays the whole of greater Portland and beyond is a local call on our land line, and even if it weren't, my cell phone service lets me talk to anyone in the United States for one fee. Television reception in 1987 was by antenna only and it was spotty. There was no cable on our country roads, nor could we get satellite reception. I had gotten my first computer in 1986, the year before moving here. It had a black screen with green letters, and you had to type in abbreviated commands for the program you wanted to use. No mouse. E-mail and the Internet were only vague rumors. Who would have imagined almost instant communication via e-mail, streaming movies, ordering Christmas presents on a computer, and doodling around on Facebook? Apparently somebody did.

Satellites fly overhead dispensing Internet service, telephone connections, and hundreds of television channels to country and city alike. Though I am technically retired, I still sometimes teach a class in my pajamas or do research through the college library, right from my own messy little office next to the kitchen. My sister, who lives in Oregon, reads bedtime stories to her four-year-old grandson in Chicago via Skype, keeping him entertained while his parents are busy clearing the dinner dishes or reading their own books.

Occasionally it seems like way too much access. But media isolation is no longer a reason to go back to the city.

In 1987, the Yamhill County wine industry consisted of a handful of pioneer wine makers. Now there are hundreds of vineyards and wineries nearby. Related to wine tourism, boutique country bed and breakfasts, small gourmet restaurants, and limousines giving weekend tours to visitors from the city are now part of our landscape. No longer do we have to drive an hour to find fancy olives or gourmet cheeses. The country is no longer as far from the city as it once was.

And yet the farmer down the road has just planted twenty thousand baby hazelnut trees. I assume this means there won't be a new subdivision on that land any time soon. The pines and firs Bill planted a few years ago are doing fine, but now that we have quit raising lambs I wonder if the sheep pasture should be turned into a hazelnut orchard.

We plan to stay here for now. Fall has arrived, and we are not decrepit yet. We are in for a stretch of good weather. Maggie border collie is healthy again. Guy is behaving himself. Pinky the cat loves us and vice versa. The chickens rule the roost, and Pinknose the old Romney totters around enjoying the windfall apples. Our old car blew out its engine at 190,000 miles, so we bought a modest new car that gets twice the mileage of the previous one. This makes me feel a little better about driving. I feel certain the grapes will ripen before the rain comes. When the rain does arrive, the lungwort will turn green again. There's always something going on in the country.

Epilogue: A City Excursion and Some Country Life Lessons

❖

It is a hot fall day in September, and I have come to Portland to drive my nine-year-old granddaughter from school to ballet class. My daughter and son-in-law work late Wednesdays. I welcome the weekly excuse to spend time with Mavis. When grandchildren live in different towns, or when school, camp, soccer, music lessons, track meets, and more fill their days, it's hard to get as much time with them as I would like.

On an ordinary day it takes an hour to drive from Yamhill to Portland. I try to start early, since traffic congestion, construction, or occasional fender-benders sometimes block the road. I don't want to be late. The charter school levies a small fine when parents are late for pick up. More difficult than the fine would be the awkwardness of keeping the teachers or Mavis waiting, and then being late for dance class. Students who are late for dance are required to sit on the side and watch. A little pressure flows from both directions.

To make the most of city days, I sometimes visit the art museum, stop at my favorite cheese store, or browse books at Powell's, which may be the world's largest bookstore. Easy access to these places is one of the things I miss about city life.

Today I scheduled a city haircut. After that I still have time for lunch at a nice restaurant on Hawthorne Street in southeast Portland. The pretty young waitress has dyed, coal-black hair pulled back into a long braid and lots of ear piercings. She wears a short black dress, tights, and black leather boots patterned with stainless-steel studs. She smiles as she seats me at a table with a window view, and I settle down to watch the passing parade.

Through the glass, I see a pale middle-aged man, wearing a kung-fu beard, a large-brimmed straw hat, flip-flops, cut-off jeans, and a sleeveless T-shirt. He is pushing a baby carriage, and I am pretty sure there is a baby in it. I see a young couple with matching red and black neckerchiefs, the kind people sometimes tie on their Frisbee-catching-dogs. Next comes an elderly woman, thin, with arthritic hands. No blue-haired granny, she wears jeans and a Grateful Dead T-shirt. An exceptionally tall red-head wearing a red dress and high heels and with a prominent Adam's apple goes by carrying a Whole Foods bag. An Asian couple passes and then a black man with sunglasses and a SMART T-shirt. I remember, SMART is a mnemonic for Start Making A Reader Today. A young man and woman carrying heavy backpacks stride by, hand in hand, wearing boots and walking shorts, as if they are off to climb a mountain. They probably are. The long-haired, long-legged owner of a recumbent bicycle chained to a rack outside the restaurant returns. He strips off his T-shirt and bares his chest to the heat, unlocks the bike, climbs on, leans back, and takes off through traffic. I see two teen-aged girls walking a Great Dane and a standard sized poodle. There are more bicycles and carriages, babies and dogs, hipsters and men in white shirts and slacks, a sunburned older guy holding a sign, which says he is a Vietnam vet and anything will help. I finish lunch, and on my way back to the car I see a film crew and recognize television star Carrie Brownstein coming toward me in the crosswalk. It's a filming of the TV show Portlandia.

I love Portland. If we moved back here we would be part of this city swarm. And I admit I sometimes check the handouts from real estate boxes outside houses for sale. Mostly I just do it out of curiosity, but I sometimes ask myself, would this house be a place I'd want to live? We could trade the farm for an inner-city neighborhood, spend more time in galleries, attend more plays, movies, concerts and readings, and drop in at the most-popular-restaurant-of-the-week on the same day the tip-off review appears in the newspaper, so long as there are still newspapers. We would also be closer to city-dwelling family members and friends, maybe do more impromptu socializing. When you live in the country you have to plan ahead. There are many quiet days when Bill and I see no one but one another, which is fine, since we are both pretty self-motivated and find things we like to do, alone or together. But city life could be interesting.

I check the time. Here's the part I don't like about the city. The traffic is bad. I consider which streets will get me to my grand-daughter's school most quickly. Perhaps I should have chosen a res-taurant on Alberta or Mississippi—closer to her school and not so much city to cross. The school isn't really far from here, but there's a lot of stop and go. The temperature today is in the high 90s and even with air conditioning in the car I feel sweaty. I have a theory that drivers, like molecules, speed up when the weather is hot. I look ahead for lane changes, swerving bicyclists, road repairs . . . I watch out for cars running red lights and count three of these criminals before I get to the school. Where is everybody going?

Hurray—I'm on time. I pick granddaughter up at school. Now we drive in the opposite direction. The route to the dance school is a straight shot on McLoughlin, old 99E—maybe six miles? We make it with ten minutes to spare. Mobs of beautiful little dancers wearing pink and black, their hair done up in tidy buns, swarm into the stu-dios. A few little boys in black go to the smaller studio in the back.

After the dance class I have supper with my daughter and her family, as I wait for the sun to go down and the evening rush hour to subside. The highway west is called the Sunset for good reason. At this time of year the evening angle of light is almost blinding on the drive toward the Coast Range. Shortly after dusk I drive out of town. As I leave the city, the traffic grows gradually lighter until I turn off the Sunset Highway at exit 57, which means it would be fifty-seven miles to the beach were I to go that way, but instead I drive south and follow the signs to highway 47 and home.

Oregon Route 47 is somehow tangled with my fate. It's a rela-tively short highway, but when my parents first moved from Kansas to Oregon in 1941, one of the first towns we lived in was Forest Grove, which sits right on 47. Later we moved to Clatskanie, where I lived until I was eleven years old. Clatskanie, near the Columbia River, is the northern terminus of highway 47. Then, after a hiatus of thirty-three years, during which I lived a variety of places far and wide, I got my job at Linfield College, in McMinnville, which marks the southern end of route 47. And guess what? The farm where we live now is just off 47. This must be my road.

There is still a little light behind the Coast Range when I get home, and I pause a moment in the driveway to enjoy the sky. Bill has just come out to feed the chickens and shut the henhouse door for the night. Another chicken is brooding in the barn and refuses to join the others. I hope she will get a chick or two for her efforts. The dogs bark and leap around. It was a good city day, but I'm happy to be home.

In the city I look at faces, at people. I love the beauty and variety of human faces. In the country I look at nature and landscape. I love natural landscape. Part city mouse, part country mouse. For now, for my landing spot, I choose country. Besides the aesthetic rewards of country life, it's an education. I have learned a lot, living here.

Here are a dozen things I've learned living in the country. If they don't sound interesting to you, you should probably stay in town. This list could be much, much longer:

- A chicken laying an egg makes gentle sighing or grunting noises. Laying eggs is not always easy.

- Ewes recognize their own lambs by smelling the lambs' rear ends, not their heads.

- Both sharp-shinned and Cooper's hawks may be attracted to bird feeders where they dive with incredible speed at smaller birds and sometimes fly off with a hapless sparrow or junco.

- Mosquito larva can develop in surprisingly shallow pools of water caught in old tires. Old tires also mysteriously propagate on a farm if you aren't careful.

- The impressively large mushroom Pisolithus tinctorius, which sometimes bursts out of the ground near our old nut trees, is also known as the dead man's foot, and looks like it.

- Flickers' favorite food is ants.

- Idiots sometimes: drop unwanted cats and kittens off in the country to find a home; turn their dogs out loose at night; dump car ashtrays on the road; throw defunct refrigerators or air conditioners into roadside thickets; think the country is a place where no one will notice what you do.

- Seedling wild apple and other fruit trees in hedges revert to old types, sometimes bitter to our taste but palatable to browsing animals. They also smell nice as they rot on the ground.

- The nicest roosters may gallantly hold back from eating scattered food until, with pleasant clucking or chuckling sounds, they have called the females and youngsters to partake.

- Juvenile horned owls make raspy, begging eep noises in the night, apparently hoping their parents will continue to bring them tasty bits to eat. I don't know if this gets on their parents' nerves, but it sounds as if it might.

- Deer can fly. There's no other explanation for how they get into a fenced garden to eat the tops off your beets.

- You can't take water for granted. You can't take nature for granted. You can't take weather for granted. You can't take life for granted.

Acknowledgments

With love and appreciation to William Beckman, my partner in morning dog walks and other grand excursions. As ever, you are the hero of the story.

Thanks to Kareen Sturgeon, dear friend and colleague, for sharing your botanical and life wisdom, and for leading Bill and me to many wild and wonderful places. Teaching environmental literature with you over the years at Linfield College was a joy and an education.

Love and gratitude to my ever-curious brother, Richard Robertson; thanks for finding and sharing our grandmother's letters, along with other information and insights about our family history.

Thanks to Kathy Brunetto, herding dog trainer par excellence, who knows how to make a dog admit who buys the dog food. I loved those Saturday mornings in the field, and so did Guy and Maggie.

My thanks and endless appreciation to all the editors and staff at Oregon State University Press, especially Mary Elizabeth Braun for her support and encouragement and Tom Booth for his help and advice. The press is a shining light in Oregon and beyond. Thanks also to copyeditor Tara Rae Miner for her sharp eye and invaluable help in polishing the final manuscript.

With thanks to the editors of these magazines, who originally published the following in slightly different versions:

"Siena." *Portland Review* 47: 1. Fall 1999.

"The Visitor." Published as "Well of Memory" in *Bear Deluxe / Orlo 34*, Winter 2012-13.

"The Proof Is in the Blackberry Pudding." *Moving Mountain: art & ideas from uncrowded places 3*. Spring 2009.

In spite of a lifetime attraction to natural history and the out-of-doors, I have a woefully inadequate background in science. I think this is due in part to gender tracking in the times when I was growing up and also to the fact that I always chose the arts in my education. I can't regret the latter, my first love, but I do continually try to compensate for the former by consulting reference books to help me understand the world. Here are a few of the books I turned to for information in writing these personal essays (any mistakes in the information presented in this book are all mine):

Sand County Almanac, by Aldo Leopold, was originally published by Oxford University Press in 1949, shortly after the author's death. I quote from his essay, "Good Oak," in my chapter "Living with Oak Trees," but I would like to credit the book as a whole with influencing my own sense of how we relate to and learn from the places we live. *Sand County Almanac*—including "Good Oak" and especially Leopold's essay titled "Thinking Like a Mountain"—is surely one of the most influential books in the modern environmental movement, and it was standard reading on my syllabus when I was teaching classes in environmental literature.

Daniel Mathews's *Cascade Olympic Natural History: A Trailside Reference* (Raven Editions in conjunction with the Portland Audubon Society, 1988) is a favorite reference. This is a clear and useful source of information on a wide variety of topics, ranging from conifers and flowering plants to lichen, reptiles, amphibians, and more.

Macrolichens of the Pacific Northwest, by Bruce McCune and Linda Geiser (OSU Press, 1997), is a handy guide that I consult in order to understand the lichens on our farm, but I must admit to having barely gotten my toes wet venturing into this fascinating and beautiful subject. Another important source is *Lichens of North America,* by Brodo, Sharnoff, and Sharnoff (Yale University Press, 2001), a huge reference book temporarily in my custody thanks to the generosity of Professor Kareen Sturgeon.

Two more of my favorite references on plants are *Wildflowers of the Pacific Northwest, a field guide* by Mark Turner and Phyllis Gustafson (Timber Press, 2006), and *Plants of the Pacific Northwest Coast* (Lone Pine Press, 2004), by Jim Pojar and Andy MacKinnon. Of course, I return constantly to my Audubon Society field guides, especially *The Audubon Society Field Guide to North American Wildflowers* (Alfred A. Knopf, 1985).

In the chapter on poison oak, I refer to Mrs. M. Grieve's *A Modern Herbal* as a remarkable compilation of medical history, folklore, plant studies, and traditional medicine, not as currently recommended medical treatment. My copy is a two-volume edition published in 1971 as a Dover reprint of the 1931 original. It was originally published to acquaint people with folk medicines and traditional home remedies when other medicines might not have been available, and I have found it to be fascinating reading.

Though I refer only briefly to Ellen Morris Bishop's *In Search of Ancient Oregon* (Timber Press 2003), in my discussion of poison oak, her book provides a remarkable context for understanding where we live. I look forward to learning more from her work in the future.